Prayerful and Playful
Preparations for Families

Sharon Harding
John Indermark

Abingdon Press
Nashville

ADVENT A TO Z
PRAYERFUL AND PLAYFUL PREPARATIONS FOR FAMILIES
Copyright © 2013 by Abingdon Press

Library of Congress Cataloging-in-Publication Data has been requested.

ISBN: 978-1-4267-6027-3

13 14 15 16 17 18 19 20 21 22—10 9 8 7 6 5 4 3 2 1

MANUFACTURED IN THE UNITED STATES OF AMERICA

TABLE OF CONTENTS

Acknowlegments

From John

Eight or so years ago, the rough outline of this book came to shape on a flight from Kelowna to Vancouver, British Columbia. Sharon and I had participated in a *Seasons of the Spirit* planning event the previous week. During the flight, we talked of doing a collaborative Advent project based on the ideas that began to take shape then and have now come to fruition in this work.

I am, above all, grateful to Sharon for her willingness to collaborate on this book so many years later. She is a gifted writer for young children, is a strong advocate for families, and has a heart for urging the church grow in openness to and inclusion of such folks in worship and in the whole of Christian community. Her hand and wisdom in those areas have deftly fashioned the guides that accompany each day's reflection on this "alphabet" of Advent, even as her thoughts contributed greatly to the shaping of each of the reflections.

I am also grateful to our lead editor, Pam Dilmore, and Abingdon Press for considering such a collaborative effort for publication, and for Pam's advocacy and then editing of this book. It has been a long journey bringing this to publication, and I hope that you find the result an enriching companion for your engagement with this season in this year and in years to come.

From Sharon

I am very grateful to John, who came up with the idea for this book. I have particularly appreciated his wisdom and patience as we have gone through the process of creating book proposals and first drafts. John has a gift for opening up the Scriptures and making them relevant for today's world. His reflections provided a wonderful foundation on which to build the engaging sections. I am also very thankful for his editing skills.

I also want to thank my partner, Peter, for all his encouragement and help. He cooked meals and looked after the house so that I could write. He was also patient and understanding in those moments when my mind was on the book and I was not fully present. Peter, your love has brought healing and joy into my life.

Many thanks go to Pam Dilmore for bringing this book forward for consideration at Abingdon Press. Her encouragement, advice, and editing skills made this book possible.

Finally, I want to thank my family, who has cheered me on from the sidelines: Your love and encouragement mean the world to me.

Introduction

Christmas Is Coming!

Is "Christmas is coming!" a statement that fills you with hope: a promise of new life, a glimpse of incarnate love, a season of joyous preparation that brings peace? Or is this a statement that confronts you with anxiety: so much to be done and so little time to do it, expectations of gifts that stagger the budget, a season of hurried schedules that seems to rule out serenity? Or is this a statement that brings something of both feelings to you and your household?

In the wisdom of the church year, Christmas does not appear out of nowhere. Advent intercedes, much like Lent does for Easter, to provide opportunity to pause, take a breath, and reflect on the meaning of Jesus' birth and the promise of God's coming realm, the two chief components for which Advent bids our preparation.

The root words of Advent mean "a coming" or a "coming toward." The Scriptures associated with this season invite us to think about what it means for God to come into our lives and all of creation. They also invite us to dream about what could be when God's realm is finally established in all its fullness and what we might be doing now to live, serve, and witness in its light. Along with Scripture, Advent is informed and shaped by traditions that provide this season with an abundance of characters, themes, and symbols. Each of these provides a prism through which the light of this season is refracted, casting slightly different perspectives as we joyfully and prayerfully prepare for the coming of Christ.

This book provides an "alphabet" of such perspectives on Advent. No one word fully captures the essence and promise of this season. Taken together, the words that comprise this Advent alphabet draw us into the depth of this time of preparation. It is our hope God's Spirit might speak through these words in transformative ways in this Advent season before you.

Getting Acquainted With the Book

Advent A to Z has been written to provide a resource for families, individuals, couples and/or friendship groups to practice daily experiences of Advent reflection, discernment, and engagement. The book will do so through daily readings organized on the basis of an Advent alphabet. Beginning December 1 and continuing through December 26, each day will explore an Advent-related word that begins with a successive letter in the alphabet. Each reading will be paired with its own "Engaging" guide suggesting simple activities that require little time to prepare and complete each day. You will find a daily Journal Exercise in the "Engaging" section for each Advent-related word. Beginning on page 115, a journaling area is included where you may write or draw your reflections.

Take a look at December 1, "*A is for Advent*." The reading comprises the opening section; and the section following the reading provides discussion starters, crafts, meditations, journaling, an outreach project, and devotions. Please note that the suggestions for reflecting on the reading have been grouped according to users (Families With Children, Couples or Friendship Groups). There are then separate listings for activities that move from the reading into other forms of response (journaling, outreach, and devotional activities).

We make frequent references to YouTube videos. Older children, youth, and young adults live in a time where digital resources are more the norm than the exception. We hope that these links will be helpful in your planning.

Using the Book

The daily readings are the cornerstone of this book. Please do one reading each day. The daily discipline of reading and engaging provides the rhythm for entering more deeply into meaning and preparations of Advent. If possible, set aside one time each day for reading and engaging the word. Early morning reading might help set the tone for the day, bringing that day's reading and activities into it. Evening might allow for a more quiet time, where the reading and activities help you reflect on that day's experiences. Midday also has its values. Please choose the time that works best with your schedule.

For Families With Children: You will need to decide at the outset how to share the reading's story and/or insights with the children. With older youth, you may be able to simply read it aloud together or to have each one read it on his or her own during the course of the day before engaging in the activities. With younger children, you may need to paraphrase or summarize the reading, according to your child's understanding. The initial conversation and craft suggestions in the "Engaging" components provide a tool for doing this. Do not feel compelled to do every suggested activity. Choose activities that will suit your family's schedules and the ages of your children.

For Adults: You will need to agree on a gathering time. If you cannot meet daily, you might choose to do the daily readings apart and commit to once-a-week meetings to share insights, discoveries, and to do (or redo!) one or more of the activities listed for that week. We encourage you to take turns in leading the Engaging elements, perhaps having multiple leaders each time.

For individuals, note that the readings have been written so that this book can be used as a personal exercise in spiritual formation through the season of Advent even if you are not part of a group. Feel free in the "Engaging" component to choose activities that you see as particularly valuable for your Advent reflection. Do not overlook those in the "For Families With Children" section. Children are not the only ones who thrive on wonder and fun.

For Everyone Using This Resource: Keep this Advent discipline enjoyable as well as challenging. Also keep the "Engaging" simple: You do not need to do every activity listed. They are suggestions, not rules of law.

And above all else, allow *Advent A to Z* to prepare your heart and mind, body and spirit, for the One who comes at Christmas—and for the One whose promised coming will usher in God's realm of peace and justice and love.

December 1
A is for ADVENT

What's coming? Ask a child that question tonight, and you will likely get "Christmas" for the answer. Or you might hear "Santa Claus": he who is coming to town and, as one song tells in surprisingly ominous language, bids that "you better watch out!"

"What's coming?" is also the question of Advent. In fact, the Latin roots of *Advent* mean "to come" or "to come toward." Advent is a season observed with eyes and hopes set in two directions. Advent looks back in order to prepare for celebrating the coming of Jesus as the infant nestled in a manger. Advent also looks forward to prepare for the coming of Christ, the Sovereign of all Creation at the end of history. Ironically, the Romans named the first month of the year *Janus*, the god whose two faces look backward and forward. Advent serves that same function, as it is the first season in the cycle of the church year. So Happy New Year to you!

But just what is "new"?

For the answer to that, the church traditionally turns to John the Baptizer as we set out on our Advent journey. From his wilderness pulpit, John summoned preparation on the part of those who made pilgrimage to hear the prophet announcing something—some One—remarkably new. But to those who thought that John himself might be the "one," he pointed them in another direction. "One who is more powerful than I is coming." He thus transformed the question of "what is coming" into "who is coming" for seekers in his time and in our own. But John also made clear that preparation for the coming One required repentance. To make way for the new, old ways needed to be let go. The journey thus was not simply geographical, not just out to the wilderness. The Advent journey summoned by John was covenantal, redirecting our relationships with God and neighbor. "Who was coming" demanded a radical new way of living.

John's call remains in place for the journey we would make in Advent. So what may be old and in need of letting go of in our time? Keep in mind Advent's "comings": the ancient birth of Jesus and the anticipated reign of Christ. What stands in your way of opening up to that ancient birth's meaning? Overfilled schedules and obsession with material gifts, which drain our energies and resources in the service of busy-ness and business? And what stands in your way of opening up to God's promised realm, the other "coming," for which this season would prepare us? The seduction of society's increasing self-centeredness, in which the future is squandered on the basis of what's in it for me now? Appeals to might makes right that leave no room at the political inn for One who comes as Prince of Peace?

A is for *Advent*, and not just because of the Christmas birth that is coming. Christ's promised realm is on the way. What will you do—and more important, how will you live—to prepare the way?

ENGAGING Advent

For Families With Children

Have some conversation about what or who is coming. Invite remembrances of previous Advent celebrations. Talk about any Advent traditions your family or church community observes.

Tell the story of John the Baptist, who was chosen to get the people ready for Jesus. Talk about his message to turn around and change your ways. Link this idea with Advent being a time to change and find new ways that help us better follow Jesus. Read Luke 3:10-14, and ask: What could we do to better follow Jesus? Invite the children to choose one or two of their responses as actions for your Advent focus.

Make or buy an Advent calendar to help the children keep track of the days in Advent. Create a short, simple ritual for using it each day.

For Couples or Friendship Groups
- If you were to listen to commercial media alone, what would you think is coming?
- Look through a local and a national newspaper or look at news reports online. Judging from the articles, what would you think is coming?
- How do news events relate to Advent?
- How might Advent address/transform what we see in the world around us?

Explore the websites BuyNothingChristmas.org and AdventConspiracy.org for Advent ideas.

Journal Exercise

Read Luke 3:2-14. What might you let go as you prepare to welcome Jesus and God's promised and coming realm? What things might be helpful to add to your preparations? Write or draw your responses on page 115 of the journal section.

Outreach Project

Create an Advent collection jar by tying a thin purple ribbon around the neck of a clean glass jar. You will use this jar to collect coins most days during Advent. Decide what you will do with the money you collect. Total the ages of everyone who lives in your household. Place the corresponding number of coins in the jar.

Devotional Activities

For Children: Make a list of the people who announced Jesus' coming; this would include the prophets, Gabriel, Mary, Elizabeth, John the Baptist. Invite the children to join them and announce Jesus' coming. Print in the middle of a sturdy, white paper plate, "Jesus Is Coming." Have the children use crayons to decorate the edges of the plate. Or staple a piece of garland around the edge. Punch holes in the bottom edge of the plate, and use yarn or ribbon to attach jingle bells. Attach yarn or ribbon to form a hanging loop. Hang the finished craft on a door knob near to where you plan to gather for Advent activities.

For Adults: Listen to the Advent hymn "O Come, O Come, Emmanuel," available on iTunes and Youtube. How do the words and images described in the song speak to you of Advent? What images are not helpful? Cut out pictures and words from magazines, newspapers, or old Christmas cards to create a montage that speaks to you of Advent.

Daily Prayer

Give thanks for this special time of waiting and hoping. Ask God to help you as you prepare to welcome Jesus.

December 2
B is for BETHLEHEM

Do you know what the town of Jesus' birth has in common with the tradition of making gingerbread houses for Christmas? Bread. In Hebrew, *beth lehem* means "house of bread." How the town came to be so named is a mystery.

Then again, why this village ends up as the birthplace of God's Messiah is also a mystery. You might have thought that God would have dropped anchor in Rome or, at the very least, Jerusalem, right in the center of attention, smack in the vortex of power. Granted, Bethlehem had been the hometown of none other than David, plucked up from the keeping the family flocks to be anointed by Samuel as the once-and-future king (Saul was still on the scene). But keep in mind: Close to a thousand years had passed since David came along. Things change; towns change. Whatever it might have been in David's time, Bethlehem was losing ground. Even the prophet Micah, who recorded the designation of the town as the locale of God's Promised One, couldn't help but put a qualifier on Bethlehem as "one of the little clans of Judah" (Micah 5:2).

Little. That assessment is preserved in the Christmas carol most associated with this site: "O *Little* Town of Bethlehem." *Little*, as in out of the way. *Little*, as in overlooked and unimportant. Few, if any, in the imperial capital of Rome would have cared a whit about such an out-of-the-way place in such an out-of-the-way land. But maybe that is the point. "Little" Bethlehem suggests that God is unimpressed with grand edifices, whether of the architectural or personality or nationalistic sort. Rather, Bethlehem points to the God who is keen on common life and common people. The kind of folk for whom hope is not proven by present pomp and circumstances. The kind of folk who, like Joseph and Mary and the magi, undertake journeys in the hope of holy promises coming to light.

Light. Like *little*, *light* is another assessment made of Bethlehem in that carol noted above: "Yet in thy dark streets shineth the everlasting Light." Light shining in darkened places forms a familiar expression of Biblical promise and fulfillment. Isaiah 9:2 attests to a people who walked in darkness having seen a great light. John 1:5 understands the coming for which we prepare in this season as light shining in darkness. Maybe that is part of why we string tiny lights on trees, and then turn off the house lights. We like the image of darkness broken by lights. We like the image of promises kept by Light.

B is for *Bethlehem*—not simply because that is where Joseph and Mary end up, but because God brings light to the most unexpected places amongst the most unlikely of persons and communities. For it is there—it is here—that the hopes and fears of all our years are met in the One who is Bread and Light for the world.

ENGAGING Bethlehem

For Families With Children

Learn and sing "O Little Town of Bethlehem" together. As Christmas cards arrive, look for those with images that could illustrate the carol. Arrange them in a special display.

If you have a crèche scene, set up the stable in a central location. Tell the story of the journey Mary and Joseph had to make to Bethlehem. Start Mary and Joseph on their long journey by placing them some distance from the stable. Every day, move them closer to the stable until they arrive on Christmas Eve.

Talk about how the word *Bethlehem* means "house of bread." Serve some freshly baked bread. Explain that bread is an important source of food for many people around the world. Observe that one of Jesus' titles, or names, was "The Bread of Life." Whenever we eat bread, we can remember how important Jesus is to us. Observe how interesting it is that Jesus, The Bread of Life, was born in the house of bread.

For Couples or Friendship Groups

Distribute copies of the lyrics to "O Little Town of Bethlehem." (Lyrics can be found on the Internet.) Read the words silently, lingering over them to get beyond the familiarities and to find the affirmations.

- What words or images strike you, in particular? Why?
- In what ways does light affect our fears? our hopes?
- Where have you seen God bring light to unexpected places and situations?

Darken the room, and light a candle. Reflect on ways in which light spills out and chases away darkness. Note that even a tiny crack lets light through.

- Where are the dark places in our lives, community, or world?
- How can we bring the light of Christ into these places?

Journal Exercise

What are your hopes and fears for this Advent season? What hope does Christ's coming evoke in you? Write or draw your responses on page 115 of the journal section.

Outreach Project

Look through your Christmas ornaments. How many strings of lights, ornaments that incorporate light, and shining stars do you have? Place the corresponding number of coins in your collection jar.

Devotional Activities

Read Micah 5:2-5. Observe that there were two kings born in Bethlehem. The first was the great King David, and the second was Jesus.

For Children: Invite the children to share their ideas about rulers and kings. How did Jesus show God's ways of peace and love? How was this different from what King David did? How might we follow Jesus' example in our living?

For Adults: How might Jesus' birthplace and its link to David (a warrior king) have shaped the expectations of those who hailed Jesus as the promised messiah? In today's society, how do Jesus' teachings challenge prevailing wisdoms about where power resides?

Daily Prayer

Light a candle, and pray for peace in the world. Ask for God's help as you try to follow in the way of Jesus, the child of Bethlehem.

December 3
C is for CRÈCHE

A crèche is a three-dimensional representation of the Nativity scene. Many credit St. Francis of Assisi with the idea, created to make the Christmas story more accessible to common folk, who could not read. In 1223, he arranged for the erection of the first crèche. It consisted of a hay-filled manger and a live ox and donkey but no human figures. Over time, crèches became much more elaborate—whether in ornate carvings, multi-level platforms that rotated when the heat from candles turned fan-driven rotors, or even living crèche scenes. It is reported that King Charles III of Naples constructed a crèche 40 feet long and 125 feet wide, populating it with 500 wax figures of people and another 200 wax animals. In other words, it was not the sort of crèche to put under your tree or set on the mantle.

The way crèches represent the Nativity preserves an invitational form of nonverbal communication. We see the figures, and imagine the scene for ourselves. The eventual inclusion of others beside

Joseph and Mary and the Child reminds us this season involves and affects more than just the Holy Family. St. Francis' inclusion of common farm animals underscores the meaning of this season's embracing all of creation. Even the smallest of children can look upon crèche figures and be led into wonder.

But there is another meaning to crèche that I stumbled upon by accident some years ago. While doing an Internet search on my family name for genealogy information, I came upon one "hit" that surprised and delighted me. Among the search engine results was an entry for a small village in the Limpopo province of South Africa named Indermark. But the entry was not so much about the town itself but its crèche: a preschool and daycare center for children of the village and surrounding area. I have since learned that *crèche* is actually a relatively common term in British circles for a day nursery or a hospital for foundlings (an older term for abandoned children).

What a marvelous addition to the traditional association of crèche with Nativity scene! A crèche is not exclusively limited to one child born in Bethlehem. Rather, a crèche can serve as a reminder that the One Child came as all children come: in need of caring, in need of love, in need of nurture. Indeed, the Child represented in our Christmas crèches would eventually do precisely that in his ministry: care with compassion, love unconditionally, nurture the very ones whom others tended to cast off whether by reason of birth (Samaritan) or disease (leper) or vocation (tax collector). In other words, Jesus came for the likes of all "foundlings" who would otherwise go unwanted.

So the next time you see a crèche, look closely at the child. Because in that one child in the manger, life comes to all of God's children—and our calling to care for all as did that One.

ENGAGING Crèche

For Families With Children

If you have already set your crèche figures on their way to Bethlehem, share stories about the crèche's history or about why you chose it. Provide modeling clay and encourage family members to make extra figures: maybe someone in the story not included in the figures, a person or an animal that you think should be in the story, or yourself.

Gather craft supplies and make your own crèche. For inspiration go to the Pinterest website and search for Nativity scenes. Invite the children to use the crèche to tell the story of the first Christmas. Do not worry if they do not follow the biblical account exactly. What new insights do you gain from their retelling?

Sing "Away in a Manger." Younger children might enjoy rocking a toy to the music. Provide a box and small blankets to make a manger. Encourage imaginative play.

Refer to the animals included in crèches as reminders that we are called to care for all of creation. Make some edible decorations to feed the birds during the holiday season. One of the easiest feeders can be made by tying a string to the top of a pinecone, coating the pinecone with peanut butter, and rolling it in bird seed. Search for more ideas on the Internet. Consider feeding the birds for the rest of the winter.

For Couples or Friendship Groups

Watch on YouTube "O Holy Night—Josh Groban" set to scenes from *The Nativity Story* (http://youtu.be/4Zh-yR0pbmU).* Or set up a crèche together, dim the lights, and play the carol.

- What parts of the Nativity story are most important for you?
- Where is the mystery for you?

---

* All websites were accurate and functional at the time of publication. YouTube addresses are case sensitive.

Talk about broader meaning of the word *crèche* and how the "Child in a manger" calls us to care for all as he did. Ask:

- What Advent activities might enable you to embody the compassion of Christ?

Journal Exercise

In what ways could you care for the Christ child by caring for children, especially those who are overlooked or left out? Write or draw your responses on page 116 of the journal section.

Outreach Project

Count the number of figures in your Nativity scene. Place the corresponding number of coins in your collection jar.

Devotional Activities

Provide a variety of Christmas cards that depict the Nativity scene. Play "Away in a Manger" and/or "Infant Lowly," and invite participants to examine the pictures on the cards.

For Children: Talk about which picture they would like to step into and what they might see, smell, and hear.

For Adults: In what ways has following the "one child in a manger" influenced the direction and priorities of your life?

Option 1: Invite people to hold their bodies as if they were present at the manger. What are you thinking and feeling? What would you say to Mary? to Joseph? to the Baby?

Option 2: Provide paper and art materials. Create your own Nativity pictures.

Daily Prayer

Offer gratitude for the Child in the manger, who came to share God's love.

December 4
D is for DREAMS

What are you dreaming about these days? A peaceful world? A Christmas table free of conflict? The look of surprise and delight on a child's face when he or she opens some special gift you have (or will shortly have) wrapped and placed under the tree?

The stories of Advent and Christmas are woven with multiple dreams. There are the dreams of the Old Testament prophets, whose visions speak of peaceable kingdoms and justice flowing like waters and little children who will lead. There is the dream of the magi, warning against their return to Herod with news of where the star-child could be found. And there are the dreams of Joseph—four of them, to be exact (Matthew 1:20; 2:13; 2:19; 2:22).

But we sometimes fail to consider, amongst all of these dreams and dreamers that form the backdrop for Advent and Christmas, the central character: God. For when all is said and done, this season hinges on the dreams of God. Before prophets and seers, God dreamed of peace and justice and compassion— and every other quality embraced in the hope of God's promised realm. Before Joseph dreamed of standing by Mary, God dreamed the mercy required of steadfast love in covenant. Before the dreams of the magi and Joseph set them on journeys to ensure life, God dreamed of incarnation's journey that would lead to life—not just for one family but for all the earth's families. And out of that dream came the Child, for whose birth and coming Kingdom this season bids our preparations.

Now, God could have kept all of these as pleasant but private dreams—never sharing them, never risking how they might be received or what they might entail on God's part. Perhaps we refrain from speaking some of those dreams asked about in this reading's opening paragraph for fear that they will not come to pass or for fear of what their coming to pass might require of us.

But for dreams to come, they must be announced. In August 1963, hundreds of thousands of civil rights supporters marched to the Washington Monument. The climax for many that day was when Martin Luther King, Jr., addressed the crowd, concluding with his now famous "I have a dream" remarks. But that closing was not part of the prepared text. As he neared the end, gospel singer Mahalia Jackson shouted to him, "Tell them about the dream, Martin." She had apparently heard him at an earlier event speak of this dream he had. So on the spur of the moment, at her urging, Dr. King began: "I have a dream. . . ." As a result, an entire nation came to hear that dream. Can you imagine if we had never heard those words or about that dream?

Then again, can you imagine Advent and Christmas without the dreams of God? I think not. For the comings celebrated and anticipated in this season are nothing less than God's dreams for all creation.

ENGAGING Dreams

For Families With Children

Have a conversation about dreams. Share stories of dreams you can remember. Laugh together about how odd dreams can be at times. Look at Matthew 1:20-21 as an example of a story about God speaking through a dream. Provide art materials and invite the children to illustrate Joseph's dream.

Make a simple dream catcher. (Instructions can be found on Dream-Catchers.org.) Explain that dream catchers were originally made by the Ojibwa people for newborn children and hung over cradle boards to filter out the bad dreams. As you work, discuss the following:

- What dreams would you like to filter out and which would you like to catch?
- What are your dreams for the world?

Retell stories of faith heroes who heard God's voice through their dreams. (These heroes might include Joseph, Jacob, Gideon, Solomon, Isaiah, and the magi.)

For Couples or Friendship Groups

Identify and discuss individuals who actively pursued a dream of a just and fair society (examples: Mother Teresa; William Wilberforce; Martin Luther King, Jr.).

- How have these people shaped our society?
- How has their faith sustained them through the struggle?
- Why is it important to announce our dreams?
- Why might we hesitate to make our dreams public?

Discuss the stereotype of dreamers as being impractical. Invite participants to share stories of times when this idea discouraged them from pursuing a dream.

- How might we change this notion?

- What roles do dreams and imagination play in our faith journey?
- How do we hold on to our dreams when the darkness seems too strong?

Journal Exercise

Listen to the song "Nella Fantasia," available with English subtitles on YouTube (http://youtu.be/HQF-l9NBtX8).* What is your dream for the world? Write or draw your responses on page 116 of the journal section.

Outreach Project

Recall Bible stories in which God communicates through a dream. Place a coin in your jar for each story you can remember.

Visit the websites Kiva.org or the Make a Wish Foundation (Wish.org) to learn more about these organizations that help make dreams come true. How might you support their work?

Devotional Activities

Read Isaiah 11:1-9 as an example of God's dream for the world.

For Children: Ask family members to suggest things that they think are part of God's dream for our world. Print ideas on paper strips and use the strips to create a paper chain as a garland of hope.

For Adults: Make a list of situations where you see local or global conflict. Write a sentence describing what each of these situations would look like were they to be resolved. Read Isaiah 11:1-9, inserting these contemporary images between verses 6-9.

Daily Prayer

Light a candle and pray for a world of peace and fairness. Name some of your dreams for the world. Ask for God's help as you work to make these dreams a reality.

---

* All websites were accurate and functional at the time of publication. YouTube addresses are case sensitive.

December 5
E is for
ELIZABETH

Sisterhood is not a theme that exactly dominates the biblical narratives; but it surely comes front and center in Luke's witness to the *evangel*, "good news," of this season. We all expect Mary, but we are first met by her kinswoman Elizabeth.

Luke 1:5 reveals that she was a descendant of Aaron, brother of Moses and Israel's archetypal high priest. But Elizabeth was barren (Luke 1:25). In the context of her times and those of other barren women in the Bible, sisters in the biblical narrative before her time, the word *barren* communicated more than a biological fact. Barrenness was taken as a sign of God's censure. The disgrace ascribed to being barren drove Sarah to arrange for her maidservant Hagar to provide Abraham with a son (Genesis 16:1-16). Barrenness drove Hannah to tears at the abuse heaped upon her by Peninnah and to prayers that a child might be given (1 Samuel 1:7, 12). The sisterhood of the barren in the Old Testament faced sorrow and exclusion daily, and Elizabeth joins their ranks.

But the mark of that sisterhood in the writings and hopes of Israel was that God was the God of life, who not only promises rivers to flow in deserts but life to flow from the barren.

So it is with Elizabeth. While her husband, Zechariah, scoffs at Gabriel's announcement of a child to be born, Elizabeth accepts the miraculous in her life with trust in God's working (Luke 1:25).

Her words of trust indicate yet another sisterhood to which Elizabeth belongs, for Luke also relates that Elizabeth and Mary are kin (1:36). Shortly after the revealing of that detail of familial connection, Mary journeys to a town in the Judean hill country and the two meet for a family "pre-union." Pre-union: because what brings the "sisters" together is not so much family ties of the past but of the future. Both carry children of extraordinary origin and promise.

For one short moment, Elizabeth takes center stage before her cousin Mary. The elder speaks first by offering three blessings: blessing Mary, blessing the child Mary carries, and blessing such faith that trusts in promises—a blessing that rightly belongs to Elizabeth as well. For beyond family's kinship, the sisterhood they share is a sisterhood of trust in God (Luke 1:39-45).

Mary's response to Elizabeth comes in the powerful words of the Magnificat. As will be the case between their yet-to-be-born children, Jesus and John, Mary's story is on the rise and Elizabeth's becomes secondary . . . but not entirely.

You see, Elizabeth belongs to one more sisterhood: the sisterhood of the bold. For when it comes time to name her child, typically the prerogative of the father, Elizabeth boldly interrupts the family's plan to name him after his father: "No; he is to be called John" (Luke 1:59-63). Blessed be Elizabeth, our sister in faith!

ENGAGING Elizabeth

For Families With Children

Share pregnancy stories and photographs with your children. How did you find out you were expecting? What were your feelings, and hopes? Talk about Elizabeth as she waited for her baby. What, do you think, did she wonder, hope, think, and feel?

Together, create a figure of Elizabeth to add to your crèche scene. Talk about the role Elizabeth played in the Christmas story, both as mother of John and supporter of Mary.

Retell or read these stories of Elizabeth from a children's Bible (Luke 1:5-7, 24-25, 36, 39-45, 57-63). Talk about the happiness Elizabeth must have experienced when she heard that she was going to have a baby. Play lively Christmas music, and jump up and down for joy.

For Couples or Friendship Groups

Read Luke 1:5-7, 24-25, 36, 39-45, 57-63.

- In what ways does "barrenness" remain a negative judgment cast on women without children in our day?
- How might the church support and speak hope to such women, as well as honor the gifts they bring to our lives and the community?

Share stories of bold faithful women who have inspired your faith journey.

- How did Elizabeth act boldly, and how might her actions model faithful living for us today?
- What might be a bold act for us to engage in this Advent as we remember Elizabeth?

Journal Exercise

Where are the "barren places in your life? What in Elizabeth's story might bring hope and even life to those places? Write or draw your responses on page 117 of the journal section.

Outreach Project

Place nine coins (or bills), to symbolize Elizabeth's months of pregnancy, in your collection jar.

Christmas can be especially lonely for those with no family. Is there a single person in your congregation who might appreciate an invitation to join your family for the holiday?

Devotional Activities

Do an Internet image search for "Mary visits Elizabeth," and look at some of the pictures. Alternatively, find a children's Bible with an illustration of the two women.

For Children: What, do you think, are Elizabeth and Mary saying to each other? What, do you think, will they tell their children about God?

For Adults: Imagine the conversation between Elizabeth and Mary. Besides the blessings Elizabeth offers, what might they have discussed? Why? What qualities do you see in Elizabeth that you wish you could emulate more in your own life?

Create a card design incorporating symbolic imagery to depict hope coming out of barren places. Isaiah 35:1-10 may provide inspiration along with Elizabeth's story. Discuss where you might place this in the house or to whom you might give it as a message of encouragement.

Daily Prayer

Ask God to help you live more like Elizabeth, who showed faith, love, and boldness as she followed in God's ways.

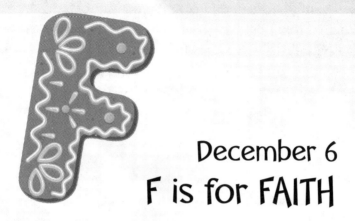

December 6
F is for FAITH

Do you faith? I know, this question is an odd construction. You might have expected the question to be "Do you *have* faith?" or "Do you *believe*?" But in the language of the New Testament, "Do you faith?" is more to the point. Unlike English, where *faith* is only a noun, in New Testament Greek it has a verb form. Sometimes we dilute this fact by simply rendering that verb as *believe*. Except that in English, *believe* does not quite capture the dynamic nature of *faith*. Unlike the Greek verb, "believing" can be a relatively neutral expression that requires no action or response on our part—as in, "I believe that water boils at 212 degrees Fahrenheit." Biblically speaking, however, faith requires an investment of self—as in, "I believe *in* you."

Advent prepares us for such investment of self as *faith* and *faithing* necessitate. Israel's prophets "faithed" long ago by declaring God's promises without guarantee that they would see their fulfillment. Or consider Joseph. When Mary was found to be pregnant, he could have publicly accused her of breaking the vows of betrothal. He believed that she had disgraced him, leaving him open to the ridicule of neighbors. But even when he resolved to take a merciful approach to ending their relationship, he had a dream that urged him to take Mary as his wife (Matthew 1:18-2). Now, Joseph could have dismissed the dream. Or he could have intellectually *believed* the dream but considered it impractical and asking too much of him. Instead, Joseph "faiths" the dream to stay in covenant with Mary. He risks investing himself in a relationship that will leave him open to the scorn of his community. He persists. Joseph "faiths" three other dreams that lead him on journeys to Egypt, to Israel, and finally to Nazareth for the sake of deliverance. (Matthew 2:13-15; 19-23).

Faith as noun and verb beckon us in this season to understand that beliefs are not neatly compartmentalized from the rest of our life, that relationship with God cannot be packaged without risk into Advent greenery and candlelit ceremonies. Faith beckons us to responsive action that, as with Joseph, dares to translate holy dreams into saving actions. To elevate our call to faith even higher, the season of Advent beckons us to join in the very enacting of *God's* faith: that this creation is worth loving and saving, because God deems it worth loving and saving (see John 3:16-17 on that point).

What it means to entrust our lives to God moves us beyond what we believe into how we live out those beliefs, especially when that living entails actions out of step with conventional wisdom. Faith in its most dynamic sense keeps us on our tiptoes, ever seeking through our living what God promises in the very ordinary corners of our lives even as, long ago, God's own faith in this world took incarnate form in just such an ordinary corner for the sake of all creation.

ENGAGING Faith

For Families With Children

Gather by a light switch in a dark room. Ask the children why they think the light switch will turn on the light. Explain that you can believe that the light switch will turn on the light; but unless you act on your belief, the room will stay dark. Turn on the light. Comment that it is the same with faith in God. We can believe that God is with us; but unless we act on our faith by following in God's way of love, nothing will change.

Plant a bulb in a pot. Explain that you cannot see the flower inside the bulb but that the action of planting shows faith in the possibility that God will cause the plant to grow. Consider giving the plant to someone whose faith has made a difference to your family.

Cut circles of card stock and print "I show faith when . . ." around the edge. Have family members complete the sentence or draw pictures to show faithful actions. Punch holes at the top of the circle and thread yarn through them for hanging the ornament.

For Couples or Friendship Groups
- What difference does *"faith* as a verb" make to your understanding and practice of faith?
- When has faith caused you to engage in some particular action?
- What does it mean to entrust our lives to God—not simply in what we believe but in how we live out those beliefs?
- In what ways did the characters of the Advent and Christmas stories "faith"? How can they be an inspiration to us?

Journal Exercise

What responsive actions can you take "to translate holy dreams into saving actions"? Write or draw your responses on page 117 of the journal section.

Outreach Project

Count the number of light switches in your house. Place the corresponding number of coins in your collection jar.

Go to Church World Service website (CWSGlobal.org). Click on "Get Involved" and then on the link "Kits." Click on "Baby Care Kits" to see what items need to be included in a kit. Assemble a baby care kit in remembrance that God's faith in this world took the form of a baby in need of love.

Devotional Activities

Read Hebrews 11:17-23, 27-30.

Light a candle. Notice that all of the people named in the reading showed their faith in God through the actions they took. Make a list of these actions. Brainstorm some ways we can live out our faith in God. Affirm what you are already doing as a family of faith. Choose one new action you might take this week.

For Children: Cut bookmarks from heavy paper. Invite the children to decorate them. Place them in your family Bible, the book that nurtures and inspires us to live in faith and to act in ways that show our faith.

For Adults: Make a list of the characters from the Advent and Christmas stories: Mary, Joseph, Elizabeth, the shepherds, and the prophets. Make a new list in the style of Hebrews. Because of his (or her) faith, (name) (action). Add your own name to the list: What actions will you record?

Daily Prayer

Ask God to help you choose faith-full actions as you continue your Advent journey.

December 7
G is for GABRIEL

In *The Best Christmas Pageant Ever*, the Herdmans—a group of brothers and sisters who are portrayed as the poster children of juvenile delinquents—take over the chief roles in a local church's Christmas pageant. The ringleader of the clan is Gladys Herdman, who commandeers for herself the role of "Angel of the Lord."

In Luke, the angel Gabriel visits Zechariah and Mary. Tradition also identifies him as the otherwise unnamed "angel of the Lord" who appears to the shepherds outside of Bethlehem (Luke 2:9). Now what Gladys Herdman has in common with Gabriel's appearances in Luke (also in Daniel 8:16-17) is simple: fear. That is, just as Gladys and her Mafioso kin strike fear in those who had hoped for a neat and orderly pageant, so the first reaction to Gabriel in his appearances is fear: "When Zechariah saw him, he was terrified" (Luke 1:12). Mary "was much perplexed" (Luke 1:29). The shepherds "were terrified" (Luke 2:9).

Fear might seem like a terribly off-putting theme for the season of Advent. Perhaps that is why Sunday school pageants (except those involving the Herdmans) seek to "domesticate" Gabriel and his angelic band. We choose the youngest and cutest of the children, robe them in slightly-too-large white gowns; and for those not too fidgety, we fashion halos out of bent coat hangers smothered in silver tinsel. Nothing frightening there!

But in a more serious vein: The presence of Gabriel really does inject a somber tone to the season that, in our efforts to be jolly or merry or nostalgic, we sometimes gloss over. For Gabriel is the messenger of extraordinary news, which is to say, extraordinary change. To Zechariah, he announces the birth of a child who will prepare the people, ready or not, for God's way (Luke 1:8-17). To Mary, he announces the birth of a child who will be king and holy—something that then, as now, might seem like an oxymoron (Luke 2:26-38). To shepherds, the angel announces the good news of peace and God's favor in a world that then, as now, seems in tragically short supply of both (Luke 2:8-14).

Gabriel looms over the season of Advent and the impending gift of Christmas, reminding us that the point of all this is not that we end up with a heartwarming observance that reminds us of days gone by but with a world-changing experience that opens us to days yet to come.

Maybe that is why Gladys Herdman is the best stand-in for Gabriel. Life needs to get unsettled with the unexpected if we are ever to accept the message that God is on the move. Even now. Even in you.

ENGAGING Gabriel

For Families With Children

Read parts of *The Best Christmas Pageant Ever*, by Barbara Robinson. Alternatively, obtain a DVD to watch it one evening during Advent, or perhaps as a family gift on Christmas Day. This movie is also on YouTube.

Light a candle and name those people who may be scared today. Ask that God would send them messengers of hope. Finish by chanting, "Change for the good is on the way" over and over, starting with whispers and becoming louder until you are shouting.

Brainstorm ways of finishing the following sentence: "Don't be afraid! I have good news for you, and the good news is. . . ." Have family members print messages of good news on paper. Display the messages around the house.

For Couples or Friendship Groups

Listen to a recording or read the lyrics of a carol about angels such as "Angels From the Realm of Glory" or "Angels We Have Heard on High." Talk about the ways you first heard the news of Jesus' birth.

- What "fears" seem at play in this season of Advent? in the world around you? in your family life? personally?
- What or who could convince you to "not be afraid"? How?
- Who do you see serving as Gabriel in your community's or church's midst, announcing that "Life needs to get unsettled with the unexpected if we are ever to accept the message that God is on the move"?
- When have you received a message of extraordinary news that would bring extraordinary change? What was your response?
- How can we go beyond a Christmas celebration that is just a heartwarming observance of days gone by and move toward one that opens us to the unexpected movement of God in the world?

Journal Exercise

How has this Advent/Christmas season brought change and revelations that have opened you up to days yet to come? Write or draw your responses on page 118 of the journal section.

Outreach Project

Count the number of angels in your Christmas decorations. Place the corresponding number of coins in your collection jar.

Devotional Activities

Read the Gospel stories featuring Gabriel: Luke 1:8-20, 26-38; 2:8-15.

For Children: Look at illustrations of angels on Christmas cards or in children's Bibles. Consider why people were scared when they first saw Gabriel. What, do you think, does Gabriel really look like?

For Adults: Discuss the way in which angels have been depicted in art, movies, literature, or popular television shows. How have these depictions domesticated our impressions of angels? What affect has this had on the impact of the Advent and Christmas stories? Create a picture of Gabriel in keeping with his appearance in the Bible.

Daily Prayer

Give thanks to God for all messengers of hope and good news. Ask for God's wisdom as you seek to bring the good news of Christmas to others this week.

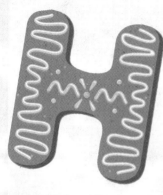

December 8
H is for HOPE

Years ago, a colleague of mine in writing and ministry told me: "There is nothing very concrete about hope, and its use is very wishy-washy." Unfortunately, he is too often right. Hope frequently does get reduced to a synonym for wishful thinking. At least when children make wish lists of what they'd like for Christmas, they tend to write down items that are within the realm of feasibility. Not too many 7 year olds write down "Lamborghini" or "all the money in the world." As for those adults who do slip into such unbounded acquisitiveness, perhaps the old song has it right: "Children, teach your parents well."

So what is it that "*H* is for *hope*" intends to stir within or evoke from us, particularly in this season of Advent? Expectation grounded in the experience of God's gracious character.

Expectation and hope are clear enough. Hope is future directed. Israel's hopes about Messiah pointed them forward in expectation. But what makes expectation different from mere wishful thinking? In biblical terms, it is the experience one brings, whether as an individual or as part of a tradition. Why did the people of Israel hope that there might be an end to exile? The easy answer is, God promised it to be so. But what made those promises credible was the experience of God's gracious character. When the prophets of Israel sought to evoke expectations of hope, they pointed to the old stories. Time and again, Isaiah and others alluded to God as the Creator of All, as the Deliverer from Egypt, as the One whose transformative power would bring life to barren places. In other words, the cause for the expectation came in the experience of God's past actions that revealed God's gracious character. Even when the people broke covenant, hope was not lost. For hope is not grounded in who we are but who God is.

To live with hope, in the best sense of the word, is to live with active trust in what God has promised—precisely because of how one has experienced God in life. To live with hope in the season of Advent is to live with trust in promises not simply of a child but of a coming reign of justice and peace. Why? Those are exactly the sorts of things God has been doing among us and within us all along—whether in the stories of ancient Israel, or the narratives of Mary and Elizabeth and of Zechariah and Joseph, or in our own experiences of God's gracious character. Hope is not wishful thinking, nor is it simply an attitude adjustment. Genuine hope remembers and anticipates the arc of God's actions and promises—and in doing so, re-orients the ways we live, and the values we hold, and the communities we shape in expectant response. So perhaps, the final word is not what hopes you hold but what hopes take hold of you.

ENGAGING Hope

For Families With Children

Talk with the children about their hopes for Christmas. What hopes do you think God has for the world this Christmas? What hopes do you have for the world?

Read Isaiah 35:1-10. What hopes do you see in this passage? What signs of hope have you seen in the world this Advent? Together choose verses from the passage to print and illustrate on homemade gift tags.

Find an attractive bowl or basket and invite family members to fill it with hope. You might print out Bible verses that bring hope, cut out magazine or newspaper articles or pictures that speak of hope, find small Christmas ornaments that symbolize hope, or use a permanent marker to print the word hope on a smooth stone.

For Couples or Friendship Groups

- Where have you encountered or been let down by hope that is wishy-washy?
- What hopes do you hold up this Advent? What hopes have taken hold of you?
- What do you see as the differences (in the world, in your life and faith) between hope and wishful thinking?
- How are your expectations associated with hope grounded in your experience, particularly your experience of God?
- In what ways do your hopes shape your life and community?
- What Bible passage brings you hope? Why?

Journal Exercise

Describe a personal experience that convinces you of God's gracious character. Write or draw your responses on page 118 of the journal section.

Outreach Project

Count the Christmas cards you have received that include the word *hope*. Place the corresponding number of coins in your collection jar.

Reach out to someone who, because of difficult life circumstances, seems to have lost hope. What words or actions might you offer that bring some measure of hope?

Devotional Activities

Sit in a darkened room. Light a candle, and read Isaiah 2:1-5.

For Children: Ask the children to imagine a world with no fighting. What would change? What would stay the same? What hopes for peace do you have?

For Adults: Describe what a world without violence would look like. What might you do to help bring that about? How does this passage give you hope that peace might be realized?

Option 1: Make paper doves. (Instructions can be found on various sites on the Internet.) The dove is an ancient symbol of peace and hope (Genesis 9:8-12). Hang the doves in a prominent place this week to remind you of the hope that Jesus, the Prince of Peace, brought to the world.

Option 2: Identify and sing a carol that expresses the hopes that Advent and Christmas bring.

Daily Prayer

Give thanks to God for the birth of Jesus, who came to came to bring us hope. Ask that God would make you into hopeful people in this season.

December 9

I is for
INCARNATION

"In the flesh." We sometimes use that phrase in reference to encounters with folks whom we are not accustomed to being with in person: a movie star from the theater's silver screen or a news anchor on the flat-screen TV. Even the best 3-D projection cannot rival an encounter with someone "in the flesh."

"In the flesh" is also what *incarnation* literally means. However we understand the mystery of what the term conveys, *incarnation* proclaims God's being with us in Jesus in fullness and wonder.

One evening in the Portland airport while waiting for my flight, I watched a small cluster of rather ragged-looking men approaching. They had scraggly beards and wore large cowboy hats that appeared to have found a home too long on the range. But then, as they neared, I recognized one of the men. It was Willie Nelson. The clothes and appearances suddenly made sense. I can also remember seeing a well-known comedian in another airport—whose name I will not mention out of respect, since my take on seeing him in person was: W*ow, he really is short*!

Those stories bring up two issues related to encountering folks "in the flesh" and to the incarnate "in the flesh" event that is at the core of this season's hopes. First, until recognized, such "in the flesh" meetings of others we are used to seeing elsewhere and at a distance might seem odd and out of place. Stetsons and trail jeans and dusters in the midst of business suits and leisure wear? That's odd—but far less odd than the One who came to incarnate this season's promises suddenly appearing in a feeding trough of a backwater town. Second, "in the flesh" encounters may surprise us with something we hadn't really grasped about the one we finally meet face-to-face. We may note of celebrities how short or tall, how thin or fat, they actually are as compared to our former perceptions of them "at a distance." As to this season: It is not until we encounter the sight of the Incarnate One found not in a palace but in the equivalent of a barn that we grasp God's utterly self-emptying love.

As others have remarked, the Incarnation asserts how out of our control God's remarkable and majestic gift of grace truly is. We do not own and thus cannot withhold from anyone the Incarnate One, or his incarnation of God's grace. In addition, we are called to care for and nurture the Incarnate One, and his incarnation of God's grace, in our lives and in the lives of those we encounter. For incarnation is the way God chose in Jesus, and the way God chooses through us, to bring love and grace "in the flesh" to all of creation. Can you believe this "in the flesh" God? And more important, how can you embody that?

ENGAGING Incarnation

For Families With Children

Provide a doll for young children to hold and rock. Sing a song about the baby Jesus, such as "Jesus Came a Child Like Me" or "Away in a Manger." Express amazement that God came into the world as a tiny baby.

If you have a crèche, invite the children to help you carefully wrap the figure of Jesus in tissue paper and tie it with a ribbon. Place the wrapped figure in a special place to be unwrapped on Christmas Day.

For Couples or Friendship Groups

Go to the website ResoundWorship.org, and download a free copy of the song "On Christmas Day," by Matt Osgood. The song can also be found on YouTube: "On Christmas Day (Christmas Worship Song)" (http://youtu.be/MrvwDGfTk4I).* Listen to the song.

• What phrases in this song stood out for you? Why?
Read John 1:1-16 and Philippians 2:5-11.
• What does the Incarnation mean to you?
• When has the wonder of the Incarnation moved you to praise?
• What surprising "in the flesh" encounters with the Jesus of the Gospels have shown you unexpected things about God?
• When have you encountered God's love and grace embodied through the actions and words of others?

Journal Exercise

What about God's love and grace fills you with wonder? How might you embody this aspect of God in your dealings with others? Write or draw your responses on page 119 of the journal section.

---

* All websites were accurate and functional at the time of publication. YouTube addresses are case sensitive.

Outreach Project

Count the number of decorations, or cards received, that show the baby in the manger. Place the corresponding number of coins in your collection jar.

Devotional Activities

If possible, go outside in the evening to do some stargazing. Alternatively, view images from the Hubble telescope on the Internet.

Read John 1:1-16. Express awe that God, who created the stars and the whole universe, came into the world as a tiny baby. Jesus came as one of us so that we could see God with our own eyes.

For Children: Ask them to talk about the ways they feel God's presence and know that God is with them.

For Adults: Compare John's account of Jesus' birth to the birth narratives in the other Gospels? Why is it important to hear all of these stories?

Option 1: Create a Nativity play or a slide show based on the reading from John's Gospel.

Option 2: Make and decorate paper lanterns. (Instructions can be found on the Internet.) Thread them on a string of Christmas lights and hang them up. Turn the lights on each night as a reminder of Jesus, who came to be the light of the world.

Daily Prayer

Light a candle. Give thanks for the light of Christ that shines in our lives. Ask God to show you ways to share the light of Christ with others.

December 10
J is for JUSTICE

"Justice" might seem an odd and unsettling incursion into the season of Advent. The word seems so, well, politicized. Shouldn't we keep our preparations for Christmas free and clear of such matters so that we might nestle comfortably in candlelit warmth and innocent celebration?

We probably should, actually, except for one problem: God. For when God speaks through prophets of promised times and comings, justice keeps poking its head and priority through the cracks. When Isaiah 9 heralds the child who will be born for us, the child is designated as "Prince of Peace," whose reign is said to be established and upheld with justice (9:7). Barely two chapters later, Isaiah prefaces the vision of a peaceable kingdom led by a little child with that of a vision of ideal kingship that includes righteous judgment on behalf of the poor and equity for the meek (11:4). Even Mary's song of praise, for the promise of the child within her, sang notes of God's justice for poor and lowly ones (Luke 1:52-53).

Justice is not that which ought to be avoided in this season, for fear of upsetting societal or congregational apple carts. Rather, justice is precisely what God announces as both promised gift and commissioned task for those who rejoice in the Christ child.

What is the justice that God weaves into this season as both hope and vocation? Justice seeks what is right and good: for another, for one's community, and indeed for the whole of creation. Justice is humbling, because we can never reduce the "right" or "good" to our own personal perspectives or prejudices. Justice is empowering, because it offers the assurance that even when the right and good seem, at best, on the defensive and in jeopardy among us, God's promised justice will not be deterred forever. Justice is worthy of the struggle in the meantime.

Now, while this all seems very grown up and complex, the frequent Biblical linkage of promises of justice with children, particularly those promises we latch on to in the season of Advent, reflects the essential simplicity of justice. Even young children bring an elemental awareness of that which is fair and that which is good. Not yet hindered by indoctrinations into what is and isn't possible, young children cannot see why justice cannot be done.

As we get older, we tend to protest that life is more complicated than that, that there are many factors that go into determining what is right and good and what is wrong and harmful. But perhaps we need to spend more time with younger children to be reminded that "do unto others as you would have them do unto you" is an excellent starting point for understanding our calling to do that which is just. We also need to remember that the Teacher of those words is the very One whose birth came swaddled in the cloths of justice.

ENGAGING Justice

For Families With Children

Darken the room. Light a candle; and read Isaiah 9:2, 6-7. Recall that during Advent, we are waiting for God's promises of a world of fairness and love to become real. Invite family members to suggest things that they believe are part of God's ways of fairness and love. Pray together, asking God to help you make the dream of a fair world become real.

Look at the websites of children who have been working toward a fairer world. You can find information at the website KidsAreHeroes.org. Consider the history of organizations such as the Ladybird Foundation (TheLadybirdFoundation.org), Free the Children (FreeTheChildren.com), Kids Helping Kids (KidsHelpingKids.org). Look at what motivated the young founders of these organizations. Observe that they all started with small acts of justice. Ask: What could we do as a family to help others and make the world a fairer place?

For Couples or Friendship Groups

Read Isaiah 9:2-7; 11:1-9.

- What might God's justice look like in today's world?
- How can we help bring God's justice near?
- What role does justice have in the decisions of your household?
- Tell of times when what was right and good seemed to be in jeopardy. What helped you to keep on with the struggle?
- Why, do you think, do we lose the childlike understanding of what is fair and good?
- How can we reclaim the essential simplicity of justice in our lives?

Journal Exercise

When have you chosen what is right and good for another, for your community, for creation, over what is expedient or practical? Write or draw your responses on page 119 of the journal section.

Outreach Project

Talk about the ways in which our gifts (both monetary and talents) can help bring God's ways of love and fairness to life. If you have not been supporting an outreach project this Advent, consider what you might do.

Devotional Activities

Read Luke 1:47-55. If you have younger children, you may choose to set Mary's song in context by retelling the story of Mary's visiting Elizabeth.

For Children: Make horns to help announce the good news with Mary. Provide large clean plastic bottles with lids removed and bottoms cut off. Alternatively, make horns by rolling up construction paper into a cone shape and taping it in place. Let the children decorate the horns with stickers and tie ribbons on to bottle necks. Have the children try singing and talking through their horns, trying loud voices and whispering voices. Ask: What do you want to tell the world about God's dreams for a fair world?

For Adults: How does Mary's song turn the social order upside down? What word or phrase jumps out at you? Why? Write your own song of praise and justice.

Daily Prayer

Give thanks for the places where justice shines brightly. Ask God to help you create justice in the places where it is needed.

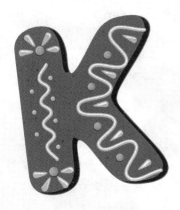

December 11
K is for KINGS

"Glory to the newborn King!" If this phrase sounds familiar, it is for good reason. Those words serve as the closing refrain sung at the end of each stanza of "Hark! The Herald Angels Sing." Advent prepares us for the birth of a king.

But what kind of a sovereign has Jesus been born to be? The hopes associated with King Jesus draw deeply on expectations and disappointments surrounding rulers in the Old Testament. The emphasis on Jesus' Davidic heritage owes to the idealized King David, he to whom the promise of a throne that "shall be established forever" (2 Samuel 7:16) was made. Yet even David had his failings, as revealed in his adultery with Bathsheba and his role in the death of her husband. The prophets of Israel criticized the failures of Israel's kings, which included personal moral weakness and abuse of power against their own people, the very ones for whom they were responsible. Ezekiel 34, for example, gives a scorching indictment of Israel's "shepherds" (a euphemism for kings). Even so, the prophets pointed to God's redemptive action through promises of kings. The child "born for us" in Isaiah 9:6 is wrapped in the mantle of kingly authority and justice. Likewise, Jeremiah 33:14-16 envisions a righteous successor to David's throne.

Those prophecies make clear the character of sovereignty to which Jesus had been born.

Justice and righteousness loom large. The shepherd imagery of kings reveals the importance of care and feeding. The passage referenced from Isaiah 9 in the previous paragraph strongly links the reign of Jesus with the promise of a "Prince of Peace." To such ends and for such actions has Jesus been born as the newborn King.

But there is one more thread of kingship that looms large in the Advent and Christmas narrative. Newborn kings are not always welcomed by old-regime kings. In Matthew 2, we see that news of a rival did not please the King Herod. For Herod, the possession of power was all that mattered; and the retention of power at any cost became the rationale for his ordering the execution of Bethlehem's children. Kings can be ruthless.

Jesus reigns in stark contrast. Power for this king and in his kingdom is expressed not in self-serving and self-aggrandizing actions: "Whoever wishes to become great among you must be your servant" (Mark 10:43). Kings must be servants.

Even at the beginning, the Gospels put the choice before us: Which king and which kingdom will we choose to follow? Which example of power will we defer to, or emulate? There are clear differences in the rules and powers exercised among us—and too often, inflicted upon us. King Herod and King Jesus make that clear. Whose way will you choose, and whose glory will you sing?

ENGAGING Kings

For Families With Children

Learn and sing "Hark! The Herald Angels Sing" together. Create some actions to accompany the refrain. Talk about what *herald* means and what a herald does.

Make small crown ornaments. For each crown, cut a short tube about 2 inches in length from paper towel core. Cut shapes along one edge of the tube to create the top of a fancy crown. Decorate the crown as you choose. Cut a piece of thin ribbon and attach it to the inside of the crown to create a loop to hang the ornament.

For Couples or Friendship Groups

Read Matthew 2. Compare and contrast the ways in which Herod and Jesus expressed their sovereignty.

- What does it look like to emulate the Kingdom ideals of Jesus?
- Where do you see Herod's kingship at play in the world?
- Where do you see Jesus' kingdom in the world?
- What is hard about following Jesus and the ways of his kingdom?
- In what ways do our observances in Advent and celebrations of Christmas point to or get in the way of,the reign of King Jesus?

Journal Exercise

Listen to the song "Hark! The Herald Angels Sing" In what ways might you serve as a "herald" of Jesus' kingdom and its qualities embodied in his life and teachings? Write or draw your responses on page 120 of the journal section.

Outreach Project

Challenge family members to see how many Advent and Christmas carols they can find that mention Jesus or Christ the king. Place one coin in your jar for each song found.

Devotional Activities

Listen to the song "A Prince Is Born," by Graham Kendrick, available on iTunes and YouTube. Read Philippians 2:6-11.

For Children: Ask the children to tell you what they have learned about kings and queens from stories, movies, and news reports. Comment that when Jesus was born, the people were waiting for a new king; but they weren't expecting him to be like Jesus. He wasn't born in a palace; he didn't wear a gold crown, sit on a throne, or order people around. Ask:

What kinds of things did Jesus do as a king?

How might those things help us understand how we might serve King Jesus in our lives?

Comment that Jesus was a very different kind of king. Make paper crowns. Instructions for various paper crowns can be found on the Internet. Wear the crowns as a reminder to love and help others like Jesus did.

For Adults: Talk about how Philippians 2:6-11 might invert our understandings of "king/ruler" and about what it might mean for us to live as citizens of Jesus' realm.

How might the Philippians reading offer a transformative "heralding" of how power is to be exercised in the community that follows King Jesus?

Daily Prayer

Pray for those who are in positions of power and authority—in the church, in nations, in our lives—that they (and we) might reflect the qualities of love and justice and compassion that are integral to the reign of King Jesus.

December 12
L is for LOVE

"Love, the Guest, is on the way." Eleanor Farjeon wrote those words as the refrain to the first verse of her Christmas carol "People, Look East." They offer a revealing connection between the gift of love that is the heart of this season and our practice of hospitality to that gift.

How hospitable are we to Love, the Guest, who is on our way in Advent? Consider the different kinds of hospitality at work in the Gospel's infancy stories. Luke 2:7 records the tradition of Jesus' birth in a manger "because there was no place for them in the inn." While Luke sheds no light on who conveys no room, Christmas pageants traditionally convict an unnamed innkeeper as the one inhospitable to Love, the Guest. It could be argued that the alleged innkeeper did not know that he turned away Love, the Guest. Then again, the grownup Jesus told a story that taught the way we treat the least of these is actually the way we treat him (Matthew 25:31-40). "If I had only known that it was Jesus" is thus ruled out as justifying the denial of hospitality. Matthew 2 records a terrible response to Love, the Guest. When King Herod learns of a newborn king, he does not hospitably order the refitting of a palace room into a nursery. Love, the Guest, is welcomed by

Herod with the dispatching of a death squad. As there was no room in the inn, there was even less room in the palace.

Consider, by contrast, the hospitality of shepherds to Love, the Guest. Initially frightened out of their wits by the messenger, the shepherds make haste in response to the message that a Savior is born. The angels praise God and offer a blessing of peace. In spite of responsibilities to keep watch over their flocks by night, the shepherds embrace the even greater responsibility to welcome the Child born for them and for all (Luke 2:8-20). Likewise, the magi follow a star in order to extend hospitality to Love, the Guest, (Matthew 2:1-12).

How hospitable are we to Love, the Guest, whose birth we are preparing to celebrate? The above stories offer some insights. Hospitality to and the practice of love are inextricably bound together. The shepherds and magi reveal that being hospitable to Love, the Guest, may mean interrupting even cherished routines for the sake of welcoming the Christ who comes to us. We may be overwhelmed by the season's crowds and by our holiday schedules and find ourselves too busy to welcome Jesus. The shepherds and the magi show us that we can choose to set everything aside in order to welcome the season's gift. Jesus' parable in Matthew 25 reminds us "just as you did it to one of the least of these who are members of my family, you did it to me." Love is not simply the gift God brings at Christmas. Love is the vocation to which God calls us. Love, the Guest, is on the way. Let us welcome and let us practice God's incarnate love.

ENGAGING Love

For Families With Children

Create a manger from a cardboard box. Provide shredded paper or clean hay. Explain that every time we love and care for others, we welcome Jesus into our lives. Ask the children to suggest ways that they might show love and care. For each suggestion, have them scoop a double handful of "hay" into the manger. On Christmas Eve, place a swaddled baby doll into the prepared manger.

Use heart-shaped cookie cutters to cut out hearts from play dough. Poke a hole in the top of each heart and leave the heart to dry. Decorate the hearts and spray them with varnish if you choose. Hang these symbols of love all over the house as a reminder to follow God's loving ways.

For Couples or Friendship Groups

Read Matthew 25:31-40.

- How could this parable change the way we practice Advent and Christmas?
- Why is it so easy to get caught up in the season's busyness?
- What cherished traditions could you let go in order to welcome Christ?

Go to to the website AdventConspiracy.org. Click on the "Intro" link and watch the promo video. Ask:

- How does this approach empower us to practice the vocation of love?
- What about your practice of Advent do you feel called to change?

Journal Exercise

Think about your schedule in the last few weeks. What changes could you make in order to embody the welcome of the shepherds and magi? Write or draw your responses on page 120 of the journal section.

Outreach Project

Read Matthew 25:31-40. Brainstorm ways you could feed the hungry, provide water to the thirsty, welcome a stranger, clothe the naked, care for the sick, and visit the prisoner. Choose one action to take this week.

Devotional Activities

Listen to the song "People, Look East," by Eleanor Farjeon, available on iTunes and YouTube. Then read or retell Jesus' story in Matthew 25:31-40.

For Children: Jesus' parable reminds us that when we love and care for others, we welcome Jesus into our lives. Cut many large hearts from cardstock. Punch two holes in each heart and thread yarn through to create a garland. Decorate the hearts if you choose. As you craft, tell affirmation stories about times you saw family members show love and care.

For Adults: Create a list of those people who are marginalized in our society. Rewrite Jesus' parable to reflect this list. For example, "I was bullied and you stood up for me." Read the new parable and provide a brief time of silent reflection. Ask: How will you welcome Love, the Guest?

Daily Prayer

Offer thanks for the great gift of love that God gave us in Jesus. Ask for God's help as you go out to show that love to others and welcome Jesus.

December 13
M is for MARY

An unwed, pregnant teenager: That is not the usual description of Mary the mother of Jesus. We sometimes want to avoid those scandals of Mary's identity. We emphasize her status as betrothed, one promised in marriage; but betrothal still isn't marriage, for the couple does not yet live together. We try to soften the reality of her physical condition by the euphemism of "with child," but pregnant is pregnant. And teenager? Customs for betrothal in that day made it not only possible but also likely that Mary was in her mid- or even early teens.

Yet this unwed, pregnant teenager named Mary is described in Luke as favored of God (1:30), given to thoughtful reflection (1:29; 2:19), trusting in God (1:45), and a faithful practitioner of Judaism (2:22-24, 41-42). Mary's faith comes full circle when Acts 1:14 includes her among the followers of Jesus after his ascension.

No wonder, then, that Mary serves as a role model of faith to women and men, and as a champion of such trust in God that does not merely transform her but brings God's gracious transformation to the whole of creation through her remarkable willingness to allow God free rein in her life. ("Let it be with me according to your word"—Luke 1:38.)

The gracious character of God's choice of her apparently was not lost on Mary. When she visits her cousin Elizabeth, she praises God in a song identified as the Magnificat (from its first word in the Latin translation of the Bible) in Luke 1:46-55. In this song, Mary expands the life-changing and world-turned-upside-down character of God's grace into a celebration of what God does for *all* lowly ones. God lifts up lowly ones. God fills hungry ones. God keeps promises.

We sometimes hear or read about child prodigies in music or math. Listening to Mary's song, we encounter a teenage prodigy in faith. For one so tender in years and experience brings a stunning witness that most of her elders then—and many today—fail to grasp. Namely, that God is truly among us, transforming the world for the sake of justice, goodness, and compassion. And that such transformation does not wait upon the typically glacial movement of great powers or famous leaders or church institutions. Rather, such transformation begins in the willingness of one ordinary person to say yes and then, to live "yes." Even an unwed, pregnant teenager. Or even us. Let it be with us according to God's Word.

ENGAGING Mary

For Families With Children

Retell or read from a children's Bible the stories about Mary from Luke 1. Provide simple costumes and props. Invite the children to dress up and play-act the stories.

Use fine-tipped permanent markers to write the words of Mary recorded in Luke 1:38 onto a light colored ribbon. Wind the ribbon around the Christmas tree. If you want a longer garland, write Mary's words several times over.

Look at your Christmas decorations and cards. Each time you find one that depicts Mary, jump up and down and say: "I am the Lord's servant! Let it happen as you have said!"

For Couples or Friendship Groups

Read Luke 1:26-56.

- Who is Mary to you?
- Why, do you think, did God choose Mary? Why, do you think, did Mary choose to trust God?
- What does Mary's song tell us about the upside-down character of God?
- What would a world that operated on the principles of Mary's song look like?
- What might God call us to do if Mary's song led us to say to God this day, "I am the Lord's servant! Let it happen as you have said!"

Journal Exercise

Read Luke 1:26-38. Reflect on what God asked Mary to give up and the blessings she received in return. What is God asking you to do? What is holding you back? Write or draw your responses on page 121 of the journal section.

Outreach Project

Look at the Advent outreach projects you have supported as a family. Celebrate how these projects are helping to bring about the world which Mary's song envisioned.

Go to the website Kiva.org to find a project to support. Pray that God would use your microloan to lift up the recipients.

Devotional Activities

Read or retell the story of the angel appearing to Mary. You might also watch a YouTube video of the song "Breath of Heaven," by Amy Grant. (Preview any videos ahead of time, as some contain crucifixion scenes that are unsuitable for children.)

For Children: Talk about the job that God asked Mary to do. Comment that, just like Mary, we are special to God and we can serve God in our own way. Provide art materials, and invite the children to create self-portraits. Talk about the things God might ask us to do. Add speech bubbles to the portraits with these or similar words: "I am the Lord's Servant."

For Adults: Discuss the fears Mary might have had when she heard the angel's message. What tasks might God be calling us to do today? Talk about the fears that might prevent us from saying, yes. Imagine what words of encouragement Mary might offer to us today. Write down or roleplay the conversation.

Daily Prayer

Ask God to help you be more like Mary, whose faith and love changed the whole world.

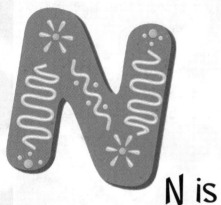

December 14
N is for NAMES

What's in a name? Names can tell us who we have come from. My own first and middle names, for example, are my father's except in reverse order. Names sometimes indicate what we look like (Erik the Red) or where we came from. My family tree sprouts one Johann Inderoldinghausermark. Perhaps his parents sought to distinguish their little Johann from other little Johann Indermarks by inserting his town of birth into the name. Gratefully, subsequent generations stayed with Indermark.

In the biblical witness, names often take on even greater meaning. The very name of God, disclosed to Moses at the burning bush, conveys mystery and meanings related to the verb "to be." Thus, God is "I am who I am" or the One who "causes to be." (Exodus 3:13-15). The name Jacob is a play on the word *heel* and means "he takes by the heel" or "he supplants" (Genesis 25:24-26). Later, his name is changed to Israel, which means "one who strives with God" (Genesis 32:27).

The stories of Advent bring the revelatory nature of names to the fore. Joseph is told that Mary's as yet unborn child will fulfill

Isaiah's promise of Immanuel: a name that means "God with us" (Matthew 1:23). Both Joseph and Mary are told, prior to the birth, to name their child Jesus. "Jesus" is an English rendering of the Hebrew name Yeshua, which also happens to be the origin of the name Joshua (Matthew 1:21; Luke 1:31). And what does Jesus/Yeshua/Joshua mean? It means "God saves." As Joshua led the Hebrew people from wilderness wandering into the promised land, so is Jesus aptly named the one who would save God's people. Whether the wilderness is formed by sin or injustice; whether the wandering results from political tumult or inner chaos: Jesus comes to do what his name speaks. Save.

Advent celebrates other names. Jesus Christ does not indicate Jesus' family name was Christ. Christ is the Greek translation of Messiah, and literally means "anointed." The anointed ones in Biblical times were rulers. "Jesus Christ" affirms the Sovereign whom Jesus has come to be and who will reign forever.

Yet another name identifies Jesus in some translations of the prologue to John's Gospel (1:1-18): *Logos*, which means "word" and more. It suggests the organizing and creative power of God and is closely associated with the Creation account in Genesis 1. The Word of God did not come as an idea or a philosophical construct, or even a book. The powerful Word by which God spoke creation into being now nestles in a manger. Word became flesh in Jesus, full of grace and truth.

What's in a name? Advent provides a season of contemplation for all the names by which the grace and works of God find incarnation and vocation in the One named Jesus. For at the core of this season is the name before whom every knee should bow and every tongue confess. Jesus: the One who saves, the One who comes in the name of the God who saves.

ENGAGING Names

For Families With Children

Talk to the children about their given names: why they were chosen, what they mean. Explain that God told Joseph and Mary to name the baby "Jesus." Matthew's Gospel also reminds us that long ago God had promised to send a baby who would be Immanuel. Jesus means "God saves," and Immanuel means "God with us." These names remind us why Jesus came.

Use hot glue to attach ribbon loops to the back of balsa wood shapes or craft sticks to make ornaments. Use alphabet stickers or cut-out letters from magazines to spell "Jesus" on the ornament. Decorate edges with glitter or other small embellishments. Make an ornament for other names for Jesus' as you have time.

For Couples or Friendship Groups

Listen to "Jesus, Name Above All Names," available on iTunes and YouTube.

- What do the names given to Jesus teach us about his identity and mission?
- Which of Jesus' names attracts you? Why?

Read Matthew 1:18-23 and the information in the reading about Joshua.

- What experiences of "wilderness" have you known in your life and faith?
- How has Jesus led you from "wandering in the wilderness" into new life?
- How and where has God been with you this Advent?

Journal Exercise

Say each of Jesus' names aloud. Repeat them several times. Which name pulls at your spirit? What blessings and callings does this name evoke in your life? Write or draw your responses on page 121 of the journal section.

Outreach Project

Create simple Christmas cards depicting Jesus in the manger. Print inside the words, "Immanuel: God with us." Give the cards to those who would appreciate a reminder of God's presence with them.

Devotional Activities

Darken the room, and light a candle. Explain that in Jesus' time, people believed that words were more than just sounds. They thought that words had the power to change the world.

For Children: Explain that every time you say, "Jesus," everyone must respond by saying, "The Word." Read the following story slowly, pausing each time you say, "Jesus." Light a couple of tea candles at the end of each of the following sentences: "Jesus was with God at the very beginning. Jesus helped God make the whole world and everything in it. Jesus became a human being and lived amongst us. Jesus shone brightly with the light of God's love and the darkness can never put the light out."

For Adults: Read John 1:1-18, and talk about the imagery used to describe Jesus. Observe that this birth story is very different from those in Matthew and Luke. Ask participants to imagine that this is the only story of Jesus' birth that they have heard.

Option 1: Create a contemporary telling of the birth of "The Word," drawing on the idea that words have the power to change the world (see above).

Option 2: Provide card-making materials and invite participants to design a Christmas card based on John's prologue (John 1:1-18).

Daily Prayer

Give thanks to God for Jesus the Word, who came to bring the good news that God is with us.

December 15
O is for
ORDINARY

Ordinary is not the usual adjective attached to Advent and Christmas. The terms we hang like ornaments on this season and its observances tend toward the extraordinary. We have our Christmas pageants or our festival of carols. Listen to the enumerations of "The Twelve Days of Christmas." We love to wrap this season with extravagance.

But when we draw near to the core of this season, we come into the presence of the ordinary. To begin with, we have a story about expecting parents. In spite of the Davidic skeletons in his closet, Joseph had no claim to fame in his own life. He was, if the traditions are correct, a village carpenter. And Mary? In her Magnificat (Luke 1:46-55), Mary describes her status as lowly, a servant.

And then, there is the Child. The coming of God's Beloved into our midst takes place in a way that is common to every human being who has ever lived. A baby is born. How utterly ordinary! To underscore the commonality and ordinariness of it all, the traditions

of that first Christmas place the birth in the most humbling
of circumstances. The Christ Child is born in a commonplace
animal pen, in a small town that was more of a crossroads than a
destination. It doesn't get more ordinary than that.

Actually, it does. The story of the One who arose from those
ordinary beginnings unfolds in a genuine love of the ordinary.
Take, for example, his choice of companions to follow him on the
way. Jesus did not scour the academies of that day, cherry-picking
those whom the rabbis and leaders identified as the best and
the brightest. Jesus wandered about the shorelines and towns of
Galilee, far removed from Jerusalem in more ways than geography.
Jesus did not call to his cadre scholars and the politically
connected. Jesus called fishers and tax collectors and politically
disenfranchised ones.

Even when he taught, the ordinary came to the fore. Parables
drawn from everyday life served as his primary vehicle for speaking
good news. And those whom he lifted up as exemplars? A
common—and outcast—Samaritan traveling on the Jericho road.
A widow who drops in two copper coins into the Temple's treasury.
An ordinary shepherd who leaves the ninety-nine in search of the
one lost sheep. A woman who anoints him with oil, while others
plot his betrayal.

Jesus' life and ministry remind us that God is with us in all of
the ordinary moments and movements of life. The birth stories,
in particular, confirm that Jesus' coming was immersed in the
ordinary even as his coming was on behalf of the ordinary. If God
is to be found and followed anywhere, the journey must begin in
and on behalf of the ordinary in life. Or as the carol "I Wonder as I
Wander" affirms, Jesus came to poor and ordinary people like us.

ENGAGING Ordinary

For Families With Children

Talk about Jesus' being born as baby, just like all of us. Read a picture book of the Nativity story. Take time to linger over the illustrations. Compare it with the birth stories and early photographs of your children. Remind the children that Jesus grew up, just as they are doing, and was once the same age as they are. Together identify some of the things the children have in common with Jesus (played with friends, helped parents, heard stories, went to school, attended worship, ate, had toys, grew out of his clothes).

Be aware of allergies as you serve some food that Jesus would have eaten when he was here on earth. This might include grapes, honey, olives, figs, raisins, cucumber, yogurt, cheese, lentils, and almonds. Explain that Jesus came as an ordinary child, to remind us that God is with us in the ordinary things of life.

For Couples or Friendship Groups
- When have you experienced God's presence in an ordinary moment?
- Why, do you think, did Jesus choose his closest followers from those who were considered very ordinary in their day?
- How does Jesus' choice of ordinary people encourage you as a follower of Jesus?

Journal Exercise

Invite God to join you as you linger over a cup of your favorite hot beverage. Write a prayer of thanks for God's presence in the ordinary moments and routines of life. Write or draw your responses on page 122 of the journal section.

Outreach Project

Offer a gift of time to celebrate that Jesus came to be the presence of God in our ordinary lives. Visit a patient in a long-term care facility, or invite someone who lives alone to join your family for a meal.

Devotional Activities

For Children: As you play some Christmas carols in the background, ask the children to help you with an ordinary household task. Make it fun by turning it into a game. Afterward, enjoy a snack together and talk about the ways God was with you in the midst of the work and fun. Invite the children to tell of times they have known deep down inside that God was with them. Affirm that God is with us in all the ordinary moments of the day.

For Adults: Ask: In what ways do you feel ordinary? Do you find ordinariness a gift or a weight? Why? Listen to the carol "I Wonder as I Wander," available on iTunes and YouTube. What is your reaction to the idea that Jesus came for ordinary people like us? What does this tell us about God? about God's love for us? Take a walk around the block and observe people going about the ordinary movements of their lives. Pray a silent blessing on each dwelling and person you see.

Daily Prayer

Offer thanks to our loving God who joins us in the ordinary routines of life.

December 16
P is for PROPHETS

A church gathers for a Christmas Eve candlelight service. What words might set the context for the lighting of candles in the midst of a darkened sanctuary? "The people who walked in darkness have seen a great light" (Isaiah 9:2). Later, when the service moves to affirming where the great gift first came to be, what oracle might be invoked then? "But you, O Bethlehem of Ephrathah, who are one of the little clans of Judah, from you shall come forth for me one who is to rule" (Micah 5:2). What do those two sets of words that help us bridge Advent-turning-to-Christmas have in common? They come to us from the prophets of Israel.

Other words from the prophets loom large in Advent's preparation and Christmas' celebration. "For a child has been born for us . . . Wonderful Counselor, Mighty God, Everlasting Father, Prince of Peace" (Isaiah 9:6). "He will feed his flock like a shepherd" (Isaiah 40:11). If such words trigger musical associations, it may be because we have heard them in Handel's *Messiah*. Why do Israel's prophets play such a large role in the spirit of this season? Some consider the prophets to be predictors with the primary purpose of telling the future. Those who take this viewpoint read the prophets primarily through the prism of the life of Jesus, as though all that concerned the prophets was a birth that would take place centuries after their time.

There is another way to view and value the prophets for the words that give so much meaning to this season. In the Bible, prophets were forthtellers as much as foretellers, in the sense that they spoke forth on behalf of God. Isaiah and Micah and other prophets addressed the communities in which they lived and the immediate circumstances facing these communities by telling forth the truth and purposes of God for their time. Christians across the ages have looked back at their words and found great value in understanding God's work through Jesus Christ.

The words and visions of the prophets bore implications for the future. But they did so for the sake of transforming the people in times in which they lived. In other words, they were not so much predictors of distant events as they were *proclaimers* of God's present workings. They proclaimed judgment to communities grown complacent. They proclaimed hope to communities lost in despair. The future mattered to the prophets because they understood that God's present workings would lead to new times. The prophets thus exercised the freedom to speak the truth of God in this day for the sake of coming days.

The prophets remain integral to this season. For like the prophets, Advent speaks its promissory words of preparation, hope, and challenge for the sake of transforming us in this day. Advent proclaims a coming reign and a coming sovereign so that we might order our lives now in the light of that expectation. Advent beckons us to heed the prophets of old and to the forthtellers and truth-speakers among us today.

ENGAGING Prophets

For Families With Children

Provide flashlights with fresh batteries. Go to a basement or a windowless room to experience darkness. Recite Isaiah 9:2 or read it by flashlight. Explain that Isaiah's words remind us of Jesus, who was also called the "Light of the World." Turn on the flashlights and see how light chases away the darkness. Exclaim that Jesus' light must be very bright!

Decorate notes that read: "'The people who walked in darkness have seen a great light.' (Isaiah 9:2)" Encourage the children to place the notes in frequently used spaces around the home.

For Couples or Friendship Groups

Read Micah 6:8; Jeremiah 29:4-10; and Isaiah 9:6-7. Compare and contrast the different kinds of prophetic messages. Review highlights of the reading. Talk about the differences described between forthtelling and foretelling. Share stories of people who have spoken words of hope and challenge into your life. Ask:
- How have these prophets transformed your days?
- When did you found it hard to hear their words? Why?
- Who acts as a forthteller and truth-speaker in our society today?
- When have you found the freedom to speak the truth of God in present circumstances for the sake of the future and God's promises?

Journal Exercise

What role have prophets played in your faith journey? What hinders you from heeding their words? Write or draw your responses on page 122 of the journal section.

Outreach Project

Hunt for Christmas decorations that use light. Each time you find one yell, "The people who walked in darkness have seen a great light!" Place a coin in your jar for each one you find.

Make a Christmas card based on one of your favorite passages from the prophets. Send it to someone who would appreciate a word of hope or light.

Devotional Activities

Read and prayerfully reflect on Isaiah 9:2-7; Isaiah 40:9-11; and Micah 5:1-4.

For Children: Explain that prophets are people who bring messages from God to the people. Sometimes prophets tell of God's love, and other times they remind people how to follow in God's loving ways. Invite the children to think of words that tell of God's love, or remind the children how to follow in God's ways. Provide a sturdy chair and help the children climb up and proclaim their messages. Consider recording the messages and creating a video to share with family and friends.

For Adults: Read Isaiah 40:11 and then play "He Shall Feed His Flock Like a Shepherd," from Handel's *Messiah*, available on iTunes and YouTube. How does the music help you hear words in different ways? Play the music again and ask the participants to complete the following sentences, and provide an opportunity for sharing their thoughts:

When I listen to the prophet's words I feel. . . .

I am reminded of. . . .

I am challenged to. . . .

Daily Prayer

Offer thanks to God for the words of prophets in all times. Ask that your hearts and minds would always be open to God's messages of hope and challenge.

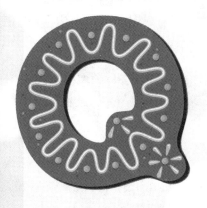

December 17
Q is for
QUESTIONS

What is that? Why is the sky blue? Is it Christmas yet? Anyone who has ever spent time with young children knows the cascade of questions they may ask. And why not? Curiosity is integral to learning. Asking questions solicits knowledge. But more than that, asking questions reveals a mind and heart open to the world and its possibilities. To be without questions is to close the door to the world around you.

"*Q* is for *questions*" reminds us that, without questions, Advent would be dreary and flat. Without questions, there is no curiosity. Are you not curious about this season and its gift? Might there not be cause to wonder, on the most superficial level, for example, why millions of trees end up standing in living rooms? Might there not be cause to question why one child's birth, out of billions and billions of others born, beckons carols and candles?

Even the biblical narratives of this season place questions at the outset. Mary puzzles over the angel's announcement that she would have a son; and she asks, "How can this be?" (Luke 1:34). Later, when John the Baptizer challenges the crowds to "prepare the way of the Lord" (Luke 3:4), they ask in return: "What then should we do?" (Luke 3:10).

But neither Mary's "How?" nor the crowds' "What . . . should we do?" are questions limited to their day and situation. "How?" and "What then should we do?" remain live questions for us in this season. Leave aside for the moment the natural questions about the "how" of a virgin birth. What about the "How?" of "on earth peace among those whom God favors" (Luke 2:14)? How will peace come to pass among us? How might our actions on behalf of that promise stem from honoring the One whose birth triggered the angels' song of peace? In the same way, John's response to the crowds' "what then should we do" evokes our curiosity about what changes and turnings this season summons from us. Is Advent's "what then should we do" exhausted in keeping traditions of hanging greens and decorating trees and singing carols? Or does John's response to the crowd's question point us to deeper ways of preparing for Christ among us? How might we share the abundance of what we have with those who go without life's essentials? How might our preparations for the Coming One transform our practice of vocation or our exercise of the powers we hold over others?

What questions do you bring into Advent in preparation for Christmas? What questions rise up in you about God, about the world, and about yourself? Ask them. Pray them. Let your curiosity lead you to faith and discipleship made fresh by this season. God has come and is coming. What then should we do?

ENGAGING Questions

For Families With Children

Tell about something you learned in the last few days by asking questions. Invite the children to tell you some of the things they have learned by asking questions. Affirm that questions are a really good way to learn and grow. Create a "wondering space" (bulletin board, empty jar, wall with sticky notes), where wondering questions are posted in the hope that answers will come in the future. Explain that sometimes we don't get answers to our hard questions, but it is important to ask them anyway.

Write each of the following words on a separate sticky note: *God, Jesus, Christmas, Advent,* and *Church.* Place the words in a circle on a smooth floor. Place an empty bottle in the middle. Invite each person in turn to spin the bottle. Wait to see which word the bottle is pointing at or is closest to when the bottle stops spinning (the bottle neck is the pointer). Invite everyone to think of an interesting question related to Christmas about that subject. Comment that asking and thinking about questions is one of the best ways to learn.

For Couples or Friendship Groups

Watch the YouTube video "What is that? Sparrow 'Father and Son' (HD).avi" (http://youtu.be/U08lAYIdZlE).* (Note: This video is not in English but has subtitles.)

- When have questions opened you up to new ideas and possibilities?
- How does impatience with questions close us to the world and to others?
- When have you been discouraged from asking questions?

---

* All websites were accurate and functional at the time of publication. YouTube addresses are case sensitive.

- How might asking questions of the Advent stories and traditions help open you up to deeper understandings?
- How can we create a safe environment for asking questions?

Journal Exercise

Make a list of questions you have about Advent or Christmas? What are you seeking to learn from them? How might these questions grow your faith? Write or draw your responses on page 123 of the journal section.

Outreach Project

Read Luke 3:10-14. Imagine that you are with the crowd and you ask, "What about me? What should I do?" How would John respond to you? Put the suggestion into practice.

Devotional Activities

For Children: Retell the Nativity story in Luke 2:1-20. Ask the children to shout "Question! Question!" every time a question is asked. Together take note of the answer that comes in response to each question. Cut out some large question marks from cardstock. Ask the children to write on one side their questions about the Advent or Christmas stories. Decorate the other side of each question mark, and hang the questions on the Christmas tree.

For Adults: Read Luke 1:26-38 and 3:10-14. Identify the questions that were asked. What were the questioners seeking to learn? When have you asked similar questions of God? What answers did you receive? What questions might you have been asking had you been Mary? had been in the crowd?

Daily Prayer

Offer thanks to God for the gift of curiosity and for the freedom to ask questions. Ask that God would open your hearts and minds as you wait for answers.

December 18
R is for REJOICE

You might say that rejoice is a word more at home in singing than simply speaking. We sing, "Rejoice! Rejoice! Emmanuel shall come to thee, O Israel," in the Advent hymn "O Come, O Come, Emmanuel." We sing, "Good Christian friends, rejoice with heart and soul and voice," at the beginning of every verse in the Christmas carol "Good Christian Friends, Rejoice." And why not? The expression of joy lifts our spirits beyond what spoken words alone can sometimes convey. It evokes notes and harmonies to sound out the full measure of its delight.

The rejoicing of Advent has its origins in such song. In the language of the Old Testament, the words for *joy* and *rejoice* are closely linked to expression in song or dance.[1] In other words, "rejoicing" comes in embodied action. Such rejoicing can be seen in Messianic texts of Israel's prophets. Isaiah 52:8 links the coming reign of God with witnesses who "lift up their voices, together they sing for joy." Joy and rejoicing are not exclusive to our end of

---

1 *The New Interpreter's Dictionary of the Bible*, Vol. 3, "Joy" (Abingdon Press, 2009); page 417.

Advent's hope. Isaiah 65:19 "sings" of God: "I [God] will rejoice in Jerusalem and delight in my people." Can you imagine that: God singing with delight and joy about "my people"—which is to say, about you?

Perhaps the most striking connection of rejoicing with Advent comes in the wake of Gabriel's announcement to Mary. When she visits her cousin, Mary breaks into the song we call the Magnificat. At the very outset of the song, Mary sings: "My spirit rejoices in God my Savior" (Luke 1:47).

Joy and rejoicing have been sung by those who enter into this season of longing for the promised birth. As Mary rightly reveals in her song, our joy and rejoicing is in God. That is a critical factor to be remembered when the times in which Advent is set do not, themselves, seem a cause for joy. We need not—and in fact, should not—be joyful for wars and rumors of war, for acts of violence or injustice that beset our neighbors or ourselves, or for the grief and depression that many experience in the time before Christmas. But in the midst of such difficult situations, in the midst of Advent's waiting and preparing for the dawning of light in what can be terribly dark times, we, like Mary, can rejoice in God our Savior. We, like Mary, can trust the purposes of God so that our actions arise because of the One who brings us joy.

Advent beckons our rejoicing. It is not rejoicing that all things are now as they should be. It is rejoicing that all things will be as God seeks for them to be. It is joy that God is at work even now, among and through us, to move those promises from hope to fulfillment. "Joy to the world, the Lord is come!" Sing it. Live it.

ENGAGING Rejoice

For Families With Children

Ask the children to list family activities that give them joy. Make plans to enjoy one of those activities with your children in the coming week.

Place a plastic cloth over the table. Put some liquid dish soap into a container and add a little water. Place straws into the containers. Ask children to name one thing that brings them joy, take a breath, and then blow through the straw into the bubble mixture. Repeat until your joy bubbles over. (Note: Very young children cannot distinguish between blowing and sucking. Evaluate their ability before letting them blow bubbles.)

Search for household items and mementos that bring joy to your family. Create a display in a frequently used space so that family members are reminded of the joy that God gives.

For Couples or Friendship Groups

- Where do you see reason to rejoice this Advent?
- When has joy come to you in unexpected ways?
- How have you shared joy with others?
- What good news would bring joy to the people in your community?
- How might our experiences of joy with family, friends, and community relate to our rejoicing in God?

Finish your time together by playing the "Hallelujah Chorus," from Handel's *Messiah*. Imagine what it would be like to be surrounded by angels rejoicing. Imagine what it would be like to experience God rejoicing.

Journal Exercise

Describe your most vivid memory of joy. Whom do you hope will experience joy this Christmas? Write a prayer for him or her. Consider ways you might help that person experience something of that joy. Write or draw your responses on page 123 of the journal section.

Outreach Project

Think about those for whom Advent is not a season of joy but depression. In what way might you offer a gift of caring that brings joy to them?

Devotional Activities

Read Luke 1:46-54.

For Children: Raid the kitchen cupboards for items to make impromptu rhythm instruments to play with music. Or hand out long ribbons to use while dancing to music. Play some lively worship music and rejoice with Mary: Jesus is coming!

For Adults: Identify and sing some Christmas carols that use the word *rejoice* or *joy*. What do these carols celebrate as causes for rejoicing or joy? List other reasons people experience joy in this season? How might these reasons for joy be related to (or deepened by) Mary's rejoicing in God? How might these reasons grow out of our own rejoicing in God? When have musical expressions of joy lifted your spirit beyond what the spoken word can convey?

Daily Prayer

Give thanks for the good news of Jesus' coming and for the gift of joy.

December 19
S is for
SHEPHERDS

Have you known an actual shepherd? Have you ever spent weeks on end living outdoors watching sheep, constantly on the move so that the flock finds food enough to survive, constantly on the watch so that predators do not snatch away the ones who lag behind or keep to the edge, constantly on the lookout for wanderers who are more apt to fall into trouble than to get out of trouble?

The first to visit the newborn child, according to Luke 2:8-20, were such shepherds. They were accustomed to movement, so a downhill rush to see an angel-promised sight would not have been out of the ordinary. What would have been extraordinary was leaving the flock unguarded. Did Jesus' later parable about one such shepherd, who left the ninety-and-nine behind in order to find the one, emerge from stories his mother told about these boisterous birth-night visitors?

Or did the stories his father and mother told about the shepherds shape Jesus in other ways? The wider community viewed shepherds with suspicion, at best. Shepherds were not the owners of the sheep; they were the hired hands. Their hands were soiled on a regular basis by contact with carcasses encountered and unclean animals such as mice and rats. Such contact left them ritually unclean, which meant that even those times when they returned from the hills, they would have been barred from worship or contact with others for periods of time. The shepherds thus stand as emblematic of God's care for all people, even and especially those considered outcast then and now: Those who are homeless, those who are challenged with addiction, those who have a mental illness, those whom we might prefer to sit in the pews of the church down the street but not our own.

Mary pondered the words of the shepherds when they arrived (Luke 2:19). Perhaps between the lines, it may be that she pondered their very presence there. Why would shepherds be the first to come? Indeed, why would angels come first to shepherds and not, for example, to the leaders of the Bethlehem synagogue, the upright merchants of the town, or even the leaders of the priesthood who resided a scant five miles away in Jerusalem?

That is worth our pondering as well. For given the lowly status of the shepherds, their generally being held as unworthy to partake in "decent" community, we are given a hint into the shepherding this child will be about when he grows up. He dines with tax collectors. He lauds the example of a Samaritan who helped a man who was beaten and robbed. He blesses the poor and the meek.

In a way, the shepherds become Jesus' "birthmark." Their identity as outcasts will mark the ones his ministry will consistently seek. The shepherds at Jesus' birth make it clear that the angel's message of "great joy for all people" will mark the saving purpose of this child's life. Salvation is for *all* people.

ENGAGING Shepherds

For Families With Children

Share stories about the ways you announced the birth of each child in the family. Whom did you tell and how? Who heard the good news first? Show any birth announcements you have saved. Retell the story of the birth announcement of Jesus from Luke 2:8-20.

Make some simple shepherd figures. Cover a small paper tube with paper. Glue on a circle face. Use a circle of tissue paper and piece of yarn for a headdress. Tie on a pipe cleaner crook. Use the figures to act out the story from Luke 2:8-20.

For Couples or Friendship Groups

Read Luke 2:8-20.

- What are the implications of God's revealing the birth of Jesus to outcasts rather than the religious and political leaders of Israel?
- How might God's choice have affected how the shepherds viewed themselves?
- In what ways does God's choice of outcasts such as shepherds foreshadow Jesus' ministry?
- What challenges does this story present to the followers of Jesus?
- What prevents us from welcoming and accepting those deemed as outcasts?
- How might this story help us overcome our attitudes and fears?
- How might some of our church rituals exclude rather than include those on the margins of our communities?
- How might we practice rituals in ways that are welcoming rather than off-putting to those not familiar with them?

Journal Exercise

Think of times and circumstances that cause you to feel lowly or outcast. How does Luke 2:8-20 bring you hope? How can you pass on the hope to others? Write or draw your responses on page 124 of the journal section.

Outreach Project

Think about the shepherds, marginalized and yet honored by God. Be the love of God to persons in your community who seem to be on the outskirts. Invite them for a meal, or make a point of sitting and talking with them.

Devotional Activities

Read or retell the story of the angels appearing to the shepherds in Luke 2:8-20. Observe that the shepherds were ordinary folks, often pushed aside and ignored by their community; yet they were chosen by God to be the first to hear about Jesus' birth.

For Children: Play a cooperative game, or work on a project such as putting together a jigsaw puzzle or making gingerbread houses. Express pleasure that everyone is able to join in the activity. Explain that Jesus came to tell us that all are welcome to join in God's realm, including those persons who are usually pushed to one side. Talk about ways to include and welcome others at home and at school.

For Adults: Print the words of Luke 2:11 in the middle of a large piece of mural paper. Identify those who are outcast, lowly, and on the edge of society. List them around the verse. Decorate the mural as you brainstorm ways to bring the good news of Jesus to the individuals listed.

Daily Prayer

Offer thanks to God that the news of Jesus' birth was sent to all, including those whom society pushed aside. Ask for God's help as you seek to welcome those who are ignored or overlooked.

December 20
T is for TRADITIONS

Decorate a tree. Bake cookies. Send out cards or letters. Attend a performance of the *Nutcracker Suite*. Lend your voice to a sing-along of Handel's *Messiah*. Worship in a candlelit sanctuary. Shop. What traditions do you keep during Advent to prepare for Christmas? What traditions are so central to your celebration that omitting them might lead you to think that it really wouldn't be Advent or Christmas for you? Go one step further. What is it about that particular activity that makes it integral to your experience of Advent or Christmas?

Traditions may be passed on from generation to generation. In Deuteronomy 6:20-25, children ask their parents why covenant and Torah are important for them. The answer given narrates the story of God's deliverance through Exodus as if it were their own experience: "*We* were Pharaoh's slaves in Egypt, but the Lord brought *us* out" (verse 21). The biblical function of tradition is not to remember someone else's past. Tradition allows people to relive the stories in such a way as to make them their own. In doing so, they shape our identity and vocation now and into the future.

Traditions become stumbling blocks when they are indistinguishable from nostalgia. Traditions are not about locking us into a past that is no longer (or never was!). The good ship Church often runs aground on that shoal. We insist on traditions in worship or education or fellowship, without first connecting them to the experience of a new generation. Then we wonder where the children and youth have gone, or why they do not value what we do. Deuteronomy has a perspective on that: Those traditions never made it to the stage of "we" and "us." To a new generation's question of why, we merely offered: "Because that's how it is."

Traditions aim to bring the truth and wisdom of past experience into this day. The best of Advent and Christmas traditions couple valued remembrance with contemporary relevance. The ornaments on our trees can sometimes tell stories that convey an ever-expanding and renewing set of traditions. This year's tree in our home holds ornaments made by my wife's grandmother when we were children or perhaps before we were born. There are wooden ornaments I made on my first Christmas away from home. Others were given to us shortly after the birth of our son. Those ornaments remind us not only of relationships and communities that formed us in times past. They cause us to give thanks for relationships and communities that continue to do so.

What are the traditions you keep this Advent and Christmas? How will you pass them on so that they can be claimed and even transformed by others "when your children ask you in time to come" (Deuteronomy 6:20)?

ENGAGING Traditions

For Families With Children

Watch the original version of How the Grinch Stole Christmas, by Dr. Seuss. List all of the traditions the Whos enjoyed at Christmas. Name the ones that the Grinch stole. Which one could not be taken? Observe that it was still Christmas in Whoville, because the most important tradition couldn't be taken from them. List your family Advent and Christmas traditions. Identify the most important ones.

Take time to look at the Advent or Christmas decorations you have put up. Share stories about their history, or why you chose a particular decoration. Provide craft materials and invite children to create new decorations to be displayed in the coming years.

For Couples or Friendship Groups
- What are some of your Advent and Christmas traditions?
- How, do you think, do traditions bring the truth and wisdom of the past into your present day?
- Which of the church's Advent and Christmas traditions do you value most?
- Which seem to be losing relevance?
- How might they be renewed, or what new traditions might take their places?
- How have traditions helped shape who you are and the way you live?

Journal Exercise

Write about a particularly poignant Christmas tradition you enjoy. What remembrances does it invoke? How has it shaped you as a follower of Jesus? Write or draw your responses on page 124 of the journal section.

Outreach Project

How could you help those who have had to leave behind traditions and the things associated with them in order to find safety? For example, contact a women's shelter or an organization that helps refugees fleeing violent situations. Ask for a wish list.

Devotional Activities

Listen to the song "White Is in the Winter's Night," by Enya, available on iTunes and YouTube. What traditions are evoked by its words and images?

For Children: Invite the children to help you make a snack that you associate with Advent and Christmas. Share the snack and briefly describe what Christmas was like when you were growing up. Talk about some traditions you enjoyed. Invite the children to talk about which Advent or Christmas tradition they like best and why. Brainstorm ideas for creating new traditions. Together choose one idea and decide what you will do and why.

For Adults: Invite participants to bring something that represents a dearly held Advent or Christmas tradition, such as an ornament, a song, or a food item. Allow people to share what they have brought and to talk about the associated traditions. Talk about what these traditions represent, both in terms of times and persons in the past and of what they represent during Advent and Christmas today.

Daily Prayer

Offer thanks to God for the rich tapestry of traditions that help shape our identity and give us roots. Ask that God would comfort those who are missing the gift of family traditions this year.

December 21
U is for
UNEXPECTED

It is a sight I have seen any number of times when walking the logging roads near our home. The remnant of an old dead stump clings to a hillside. If it is old enough, it may still have the notches used for springboards by loggers of a couple of generations past. It would seem to be as dead as dead can be. But out of the middle of that stump grows a tree. Some of its roots often grapple around that old dead stump as it reaches down into the earth. Out of death comes life. Who would have expected that?

Actually, the prophet Isaiah expected such a thing. During a time of great political turmoil and fear, he used the image of a shoot growing from a stump to represent God's promise of a just and righteous king (Isaiah 11:1-10). The shoot growing from the stump of Jesse represented the promise that an ancestor of David would emerge and establish peace and harmony. Isaiah understood something about God. God is not just about raising expectations. God is all about forging *un*-expectations!

Advent reveals that same surprising nature of God, as do the storytellers who tell the most unexpected tale of Christmas. Take Luke 2:1-7, for example: God does not go for the spectacle of a royal birth in Caesar's nursery room. That's where you would expect kings to emerge. Instead, God takes the unexpected route of disembarking in a feeding trough in a backwater town, where nobody would expect anything or anyone important. Nobody, that is, except for another centuries-past prophet named Micah, who placed his marker on Messiah's birth in an out of the way place called Bethlehem, one of "Judah's little clans" (Micah 5:2). Nobody, that is, except for nobodies like shepherds. Nobody, that is, except for a pair of refugees named Joseph and Mary, who arrived too late to secure suitable surroundings for the birth that came—ready or not.

In such places, among such people, the unexpected nature of Christmas and the God who births the whole astonishing chain of events overtake us. Christmas may still catch us off guard in the unlikeliest of places. Over a coffee table. At a soup kitchen. And the reason it may surprise us in such places is because of the unlikely ones in whom we unexpectedly encounter Christ. In the crisis of a friend who has no one else to turn to but you, will you make room for her? In the good news celebrated by folks whose poverty or homelessness might seem to void any expectation of joy in their world, will you trust with them that this season's joy is for all people—not just for the ones who have families to visit and presents to unwrap?

Christmas does not depend on candlelit sanctuaries for its surprise. Its joys may come to us at any place, in anyone, where God chooses to come among us. Are you ready for the unexpected encounter with God's new life?

ENGAGING Unexpected

For Families With Children

Invite the children to tell about times they had an unexpected surprise. Tell the children about the biggest surprise you ever had. Watch the YouTube video "An Unexpected Christmas," the story of Christmas told by the kids of St. Paul's Church, Auckland, New Zealand (http://youtu.be/TM1XusYVqNY).* Alternatively, retell stories of the unexpected news that Joseph and Mary received, as recorded in Matthew 1:18-21 and Luke 1:26-38.

Challenge family members to gift one another with unexpected acts of kindness between now and Christmas. Encourage each person to do this quietly, without drawing attention to the act.

Ask each family member to choose several Christmas ornaments and to find unexpected places to display them around the house.

For Couples or Friendship Groups

Watch the Youtube video "O Little Town of Bethlehem," the story of the birth of Jesus, as told by the people of Bethlehem (http://youtu.be/bjQDl95tOcU).*

- What unexpected insights did you gain from this retelling?
- What part of the Christmas story is the most unexpected for you?
- When has the gift of Christmas caught you by surprise in something? in someone?
- When and in what ways has God unexpectedly come among you? What was your response?

---

* All websites were accurate and functional at the time of publication. YouTube addresses are case sensitive.

Journal Exercise

When have you experienced the joy of meeting Christ in the unlikeliest of places? How can you stay open to these kinds of unexpected encounters? Write or draw your responses on page 125 of the journal section.

Outreach Project

List people who serve in ways that tend to go unnoticed, such as the school janitor, store cashier, or church secretary. Make a point of thanking them.

Plan to do something unexpected to celebrate the gift of Christmas. Maybe you might drop in on folks you have not seen for ages, or invite someone who might be alone to join your Christmas celebration.

Devotional Activities

Take a walk and look for plants growing in unexpected places. Alternatively, do an Internet image search for Isaiah 11:1; and look at some of the pictures.

For Children: Plant seeds, or place a cutting in water to root. Marvel at how God brings new life in unexpected places. Encourage the children to keep the seeds or the cutting watered and to track any new growth that comes.

For Adults: When have you encountered a plant growing in an unexpected place? How might this be a metaphor for Christmas and God's unexpected nature? Provide writing and art materials for participants to convey their thoughts in word or image.

Daily Prayer

Offer thanks to God for the unexpected stories of Christmas. Ask that God would open your hearts and minds to the unexpected joys that can come in the unlikeliest of places.

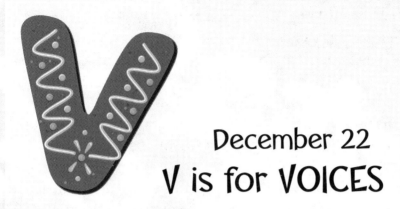

December 22
V is for VOICES

Do you hear what I hear? This year I joined the legion of folks who wear hearing aids. Initially, it was a blow to my pride. To me, the world should have been speaking louder for my sake. But the sounds of life were still there, speaking on their own terms. I just needed help. I realized that truth on one of the first summer afternoons I sat outside so aided. I thought that our community had seen a decline in birds. I hadn't heard them as I once did. Much to my surprise, the sound of bird songs that day was extraordinary. The voices were there all along. I just needed help in order to hear them.

We all sometimes need help to hear. Advent brings such possibility. The din of war and violence, depression and anger, can take a toll on us. We may find it hard to hear any word of hope, any voice of promise. And in not hearing, we may surrender to the cynicism of this time and every time: *Nothing ever changes. The world is a hostile place. The one with the most toys at the end wins.* It's not that we end up tone deaf. More important, we may end up heart deaf, spirit deaf, hope deaf.

But Advent insists on speaking. In the darkest season of the year in the Northern Hemisphere, it gives voice to new light. The stories of this season relate all manner of voices shouting or whispering their way into various dark nights of the soul. To Israel in exile, voices of prophets break the silence of despair with the promise of homecoming. To a barren couple, a voice interrupts with the promise of a child who would prepare *the* Child's way. A voice beckons a young girl to accept the incredible possibility of the impossible. A voice beckons a man disgraced by his betrothed not to follow his intention to give her up but to take her and the child as his own. A voice, then multiple voices, breaks a night's sky above outcast shepherds, announcing that there is good news for the likes of them and for the likes of all.

Mary's voice sings to the God who turns things right-side up. Joseph's voice speaks trust that defies community convention. Elizabeth's voice speaks blessing.

Advent beckons us to hear such voices as these above and beyond the noise that too often drowns out hope. The voices of this season call us to prepare not for the same old, same old, but for the new thing God is doing. And not just in one Christmas past, as in some "once upon a time" story. Advent beckons us to hear the voice of what God continues to do even now. Beyond that, Advent beckons us to be the voice of God's grace and justice and compassion in this God-beloved world. What voices will you hear and heed this season? Do you hear what I hear?

ENGAGING Voices

For Families With Children

Record the children talking about the Christmas story. Play back the recordings. Ask whether they have listened to themselves before. Do they sound different on the recording? Talk about what angels or shepherds might sound like. What, do you think, did Jesus' voice sound like when he was a baby? when he was a grown-up?

Use your voices to sing praise to God like Mary did. Play some Christmas worship music and invite the children to join in. Raid your kitchen cupboards to find things that can be turned into rhythm instruments.

For Couples or Friendship Groups

- Whose voice do you find most comforting and most hopeful in your life? Why?
- What voices do you listen to during Advent in song? in Scripture? in conversation?
- What about these voices helps you enter into Advent and hold on to its hopes and promises?
- What voices have you heard and heeded this season?

Watch the YouTube video "'The Power of Words' (Slow Version)" (http://youtu.be/JFLgyONK1Pc). Read John 1:1-14.

- What connections do you see between the video and John's prologue (John 1:1-18)?
- When have others been the voice of God's grace and compassion for you?
- How are your words affecting others this Advent?

---

* All websites were accurate and functional at the time of publication. YouTube addresses are case sensitive.

Journal Exercise

Play your favorite carol and listen to the voice of the songwriter. What is God saying to you through the music? Write or draw your responses on page 125 of the journal section.

Outreach Project

Remember those without voices, those who are unable to speak out for themselves. How can you be the voice of God's justice for them?

Make a list of Advent and Christmas carols. How many did you remember? Place the corresponding number of coins in your collection jar.

Devotional Activities

Listen to the carol "Do You Hear What I Hear?" available on iTunes and YouTube.

For Children: Find some Christmas cards with pictures of the Christmas story. Look at the pictures and imagine what each person is saying. What about the animals? What, do you think, did each person hear? Ask the children to imagine that they could go into the picture of the Christmas story. What would you hear? Create cartoon strips of the Nativity that depict the voices and sounds of the story.

For Adults: Make a list of all of the voices in the Christmas story, including the voices of the animals. Create a litany that represents each voice and what they add to the sound of Advent becoming Christmas.

Daily Prayer

Give thanks to God for all of the voices of Advent. Pray that the voices that declare God's grace and love would speak loudly and clearly this December.

December 23
W is for WAIT

"Wait: To remain or rest in expectation. . . . To remain or be in readiness. . . . To work as a waiter or waitress."[1] These are dictionary definitions of the word *wait*. More important, they are all vital aspects of what it means to wait for Christmas in the season of Advent.

Waiting at times involves inactivity. Waiting is difficult in a time and society accustomed to instant gratification. We grow impatient when a computer takes more than a few seconds to load. We grow impatient when things and persons do not immediately change as we wish. But in truth, there are some things we cannot summon into being on our timetables. The prophets spoke of a coming messiah. But no matter how fervent their hope, they could not force an earlier time for that promise to

---

1 *The American Heritage Dictionary of the English Language*, fourth edition, "Wait," (Houghton Mifflin Company, 2000) page 1934.

come to fruition. The birth of Mary's child was not prearranged to happen before the arduous journey to Bethlehem. As Paul notes in Romans 8:25, waiting with hope summons the discipline of patience.

Such patience in Advent's waiting relies on expectation and readiness. Waiting without expectation is merely passing time—or worse. For when the future is no longer viewed with anticipation, it can be overtaken by despair or fear. The hope of a new king was no cause of celebration for King Herod. He did not live in expectation. As a result, he lashed out in fear against the future. In contrast, John the Baptist waited with expectation for the One whose coming he prepared. But John's proclaimed posture of waiting was not one of idly standing by. To wait from John's perspective was to live in readiness. Such readiness summoned change and repentance in this moment. Such waiting required action.

Which leads to the third element of waiting: to live in active service. We wait *for* Christ as we wait *on* Christ. We serve Christ in this day as we wait for Christ to come. We wait for Christ's kingdom by *engaging* in actions that bear witness to the qualities of that coming kingdom.

That is how we wait in our day. That is how people of faith have always waited for Advent's promised hope. That is how the prophets waited, joining expectation of God's promises with the summons to do justice, love kindness, and walk humbly with God. That is how Joseph and Mary waited, joining expectation of God's promises with choices to journey with one another, no matter how difficult or impossible that journey seemed at the outset.

Our immediate wait for Christmas Day is almost over. But our lifetime of faithful waiting stretches forward. We wait with patient expectation for what God alone can do. We wait with practiced expectation of what God places into our hands and capabilities now. Energized by Advent's expectations, let us wait on God.

ENGAGING Wait

For Families With Children

Gather around a clock that has a second hand and have the children watch the hand move around. Hide the face of the clock from the children, and ask them to say when they think one minute has passed. Ask: How did it feel to wait for the time to pass? When is it hard to wait? When is it easy? What things are worth waiting for?

Recall that Advent is a time of waiting and hoping for God's ways of love and peace to come to the whole world. What might that be like? Invite the children to finish this sentence: "I am waiting for a world where…." Make ornaments from circles cut from used Christmas cards. Print each child's sentence on the back of his or her ornament. Punch a hole at the top of the circle and thread yarn through the hole to create a loop for hanging the ornament on your tree.

For Couples or Friendship Groups

Share stories of situations that required a prolonged period of waiting.

- What was the hardest thing about waiting in that situation?
- What or who helped you through the waiting time?

Listen to the song "Waiting on the World to Change," by John Mayer, available on iTunes and YouTube. Read Micah 4:1-5.

- In what ways is the waiting described in this song different from waiting with expectation and readiness?
- How can we wait with expectation and readiness?
- What are you waiting for God to do in the world?
- What is God waiting for you to do in the world?

Journal Exercise

Take five minutes of quiet to wait before God today (Isaiah 40:30). What things came to mind as you were waiting? What do you think

God is saying to you? Write or draw your responses on page 126 of the journal section.

Outreach Project

At the end of the day, think about the times you practiced waiting today. List as many as you can remember. Place the corresponding number of coins in your collection jar.

Devotional Activities

Read Romans 8:18-25.

For Children: Look at a calendar. Count the number of days in Advent. How many days have passed? How many remain? What has it been like to wait? If you haven't already set up the crèche, do so now. Invite the children to play with the figures of Mary and Joseph. What, do you think, did they do as they waited for the coming of baby Jesus?

For Adults: Provide recent issues of local and national newspapers. Invite the participants to clip out articles that highlight situations they hope will change. What would bring about such change? For what change would you have to wait? For what change would you have to work?

Daily Prayer

Offer thanks to God for being with you in this time of waiting. Ask the Spirit to help you identify the things you can do to help bring God's ways of love to the world.

December 24
X is for XRISTOS

Does this day's word appear unfamiliar? Replace the *X* with *Ch*. *Xristos* is simply the Greek spelling of *Christ*, which conveys its even older meaning in Hebrew of "Messiah." So using today's honored letter, one might even say: "Merry Xmas Eve!"

That abbreviation may strike a discordant note. It is routinely interpreted as an affront to the celebration upon whose eve we poise. For some, *Xmas* triggers the annual battle cries of an alleged war on Christmas because the abbreviation is perceived as an attempt to take Christ out of Christmas.

If we want to get our religion right, sometimes we need to get it old enough. *Xmas* did not originate in a conspiracy to disrespect Jesus. Rather, the abbreviation emerged in circumstances grounded in informed faith and enterprising evangelism. Since the church's earliest days, abbreviations have been a common feature in Christian art and communication. In days of persecution, abbreviations communicated the faith in trying times. For example, early Christians superimposed the first two letters in *Xristos*, *chi* (*X*) and *rho* (*P*), to form an ancient emblem for followers of Christ. You may even still find the Chi Rho emblem on your church's paraments or your pastor's stoles.

Likewise, *Xmas* did not originate with opponents of the church or revilers of the faith seeking to do away with a Christ-centered Christmas. In the sixteenth century, print type had to be handset. As a result, all kinds of abbreviations were used to cut down on both time and costs in printing. The church pioneered abbreviations such as *Xmas* and *Xianity* in pamphlets and books that were that day's chief communication tools. The priority of getting the Word out resulted in the widespread use of *Xmas* in religious publications.

What are we to make of *Xristos* as the origin for *Xmas* in our day, especially on this particular eve of Christmas? We celebrate tonight the birth of the child we identify as God's Messiah, the Xristos. The Gospels trace a frequent reluctance on Jesus' part to claim this title. But Matthew and Luke both tell of one occasion where disciples of John ask Jesus, "Are you the one?" Listen to Jesus' answer and what it reveals about his identity and vocation as God's Xristos: "The blind receive their sight, the lame walk, the lepers are cleansed, the deaf hear, the dead are raised, and the poor have good news brought to them" (Matthew 11:2-5; Luke 7:18-22).

So as you gather with others or in solitude this evening or tomorrow to celebrate the birth, with carols or by candlelight, by song or by silence, remember how God's Xristos is to be known. In restored sight and movement. In outcast ones made whole. In ears that hear the sounds of life and grace. In the fear of death overcome by the power of life. And in hope and justice for those who are poor. Celebrate those things on this eve of Christmas. For this evening's anticipation is nothing less than God's gift of the Xristos, the promised Messiah, to the world.

ENGAGING Xristos

For Families With Children

Provide examples of abbreviations that are used in everyday life, such as R.S.V.P. (please reply). Older children may know abbreviations used in texting, so encourage them to give examples. Talk about the practical reasons for using abbreviations. Explain that the letter *X* is an abbreviation of the Greek word *Xristos*, which means "Christ." This is why we sometimes hear people refer to Christmas as Xmas.

Draw and cut out the letter *X* from cardboard. Recall that *X* is the abbreviation of the Greek word Xristos. Paint white glue over the cardboard. Tear up pieces of Christmas tissue paper and cover the *X* with them. Gently paint over the *X* with white glue and sprinkle with glitter. Allow the *X*s to dry and incorporate them into your Christmas decorations.

For Couples or Friendship Groups

Invite participants to list those things that help to form their identity. Provide opportunity for those who wish to share. Read Luke 7:20-23.

- What does the title "Christ" mean to you?
- What do you associate with this title?
- Have you ever wondered whether Jesus was "the one"?
- What reassured or convinced you?
- What do you find surprising about Jesus' answer?
- Where do you see God's Xristos being made known in the world?
- Why, do you think, is the coming of God's Christ good news?

Journal Exercise

Read Matthew 11:1-5. What is the voice of Xristos calling you to do? How does Xristos's coming touch you with purpose? Write or draw your responses on page 126 of the journal section.

Outreach Project

Offer a gift of love in celebration of Xristos's coming.

Count and roll the contents of your offering jar. Make arrangements to send the money to the cause you chose to support this Advent.

Volunteer to provide transportation for someone with no car to the Christmas Eve service.

Devotional Activities

For Children: Enjoy a special birthday meal for Jesus the Xristos. Younger children might enjoy seeing lit candles and singing "Happy Birthday." Afterward, invite everyone to draw a picture for Jesus. Place these pictures under the tree with the other gifts. Sing some Christmas carols to celebrate the coming of Christ; or watch A *Charlie Brown Christmas*, available on YouTube, to hear Linus's retelling of the story of Xristos's coming.

For Adults: Listen to a recording or sing the carol "O Come, All Ye Faithful." Ask the participants to reflect on what the coming of Xristos means to them. Out of that reflection, have them write a prayer. Share thoughts and prayers.

Daily Prayer

Offer thanks for God's gift of the Christ, the promised Messiah, into the world.

December 25
Y is for YES

What is the most memorable element of the Christmas story for you? Is it the birth of God's Messiah in a stable? Does it come in angels singing God's peace and favor for all people in the night sky? Might it be the headlong rush of shepherds to see for themselves? Could it be the quiet pondering of Mary at all of these things?

To these, let me add another word of this day's stunning consequence. It does not come from the birth accounts of Matthew or Luke. It comes from a letter written to a church by the apostle Paul. The date is not Christmas, but the message surely is: "For in [Christ] every one of God's promises is a 'Yes'" (2 Corinthians 1:20a).

Remember a time in your life when what had always been a "no" for you became a "yes." As a child or youth, that moment might have come in permission finally given to stay overnight with friends or to drive a car. As an adult, that moment might have come when you found that one and only who said yes to you and became your spouse; or it might have been the offer of a job after a long and difficult search. Recall what "yes" felt like in those situations. The joy it brought. The future it opened. Perhaps there were tears or laughter or both. With all of those memories and feelings, listen again on this Christmas Day to Paul. "For in [Christ] every one of God's promises is a 'Yes.'"

Paul's understanding of Jesus as God's "Yes" is not theological abstraction. It is the distillation of Jesus' acts of ministry. When religious elites sought to keep sinners at arm's length from "decent" people, Jesus said yes to table fellowship with outcasts. When fears of contamination built ritualized walls against lepers, Jesus said yes through healing that brought restoration to community. When tradition relegated women to silent roles in the background, Mary the mother sang her Magnificat and Mary Magdalene witnessed to the empty tomb and the resurrected Jesus. In Jesus Christ, the walls of "no" started tumbling down when God's promises found their incarnate "yes" on Christmas day.

Have you been waiting for a yes in your life, a yes that embraces and values and commissions you? This day brings such an answer to you and to all. Christ is the "Yes" to all of God's promises. The forces that negate hope, relying on the despair and fear thus generated, denying the love and justice promised, have met their match today. Their power is fading. The power of God's "Yes," the wave of the future, has been born this day in the city of David. Yes!

ENGAGING Yes

For Families With Children

Ask the children to tell you about times when they were excited to have someone say yes to them. What is the best "yes" you have ever heard? When have you said yes to someone else? How does that feel? Explain that the Bible describes Jesus as "God's Yes." Make a list of the good things that Jesus did on this earth. Go through the list, saying, "God says yes to. . . ."

Younger children might enjoy singing the first verse and refrain of "Jesus Loves Me." Encourage the children to shout out the word *yes* during the refrain.

Read the Nativity story together, taking note of the people who said yes (Elizabeth, Zachariah, Mary, Joseph, and shepherds) and those who said no (inn keeper, Herod). Invite the children to run into every room of the house and shout, "God said yes! Jesus is born!"

For Couples or Friendship Groups
- When have you received an unexpected "yes"?
- When has a "yes" changed your life?
- What might hold us back from accepting the "yes" of another?
- What holds us back from saying yes?
- How does the word *yes* involve trust, both for the speaker and the hearer?
- Which particular promise of God do you see the "yes" for in Jesus? Why?
- In your experience, what walls have been brought down by the answer "yes"?
- What walls still await you or another to say yes?

Journal Exercise

Read Matthew 25:31-40. In what ways do we say no to Jesus? What is one thing you can do this year to change that no into a yes? Write or draw your responses on page 127 of the journal section.

Outreach Project

Is there someone you know who needs a "yes" right now? How might you offer that word to him or her? Consider it as a Christmas present you can give.

Devotional Activities

For Children: Cut the letters *Y-E-S* from cardboard. Make them big. Wrap the letters in a variety of materials, such as tissue paper, ribbon, and yarn. Display finished letters in a prominent place, as a reminder of God's "Yes." Share one of your favorite biblical promises with the children as the letters are displayed.

For Adult: Invite participants to imagine sitting with Jesus at table and hearing him say, "Yes." What would you hope that yes to be about? What might be holding you back from hearing that "yes" God is already speaking? What "yes" might God be waiting on you to make?

Daily Prayer

Offer thanks to God for the birth of Jesus, who brought God's "Yes" to the whole world.

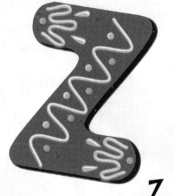

December 26
Z is for ZOE

The journey has been made from the first reading in this book that engaged us in *"A* is for *Advent"* to yesterday's celebration of the promised birth announcement of God's "Yes" in *"Y* is for *Yes."* But one more letter remains to set us off on our way of following the One who has been born for us and for all. The letter is *Z*, and its word is *zoe*. Like *Xristos*, *zoe* comes to us from Greek. Perhaps you have seen that word used only as a name, if at all. But even if you have never seen it stand alone, I suspect that you have seen it any number of times in different forms: *zoology. zoo.* You see, *zoe* means "life."

This book's final letter and word remind us of the closing and opening word of Christmas, which is *life*. Christmas is a birthday party. We celebrate the life of the infant Jesus, born in Bethlehem; and we celebrate the life that God promises to bring through this child.

We have encountered the character of those promises for life through these readings and engagements. The prophets have reminded us that the life this child portends involves a peaceable kingdom. In contrast to dog-eat-dog and whoever-has-the-most-toys-wins mentalities that constantly set us against one another, the coming of this child promises a realm where none will hurt or destroy on God's holy mountain and where those who have two coats will share with one who has none. Jesus' subsequent ministry reveals that the life this child brings promises inclusion of the otherwise shut out, forgiveness of the otherwise condemned, and reconciliation of the otherwise estranged. The zoe that Jesus brings is not limited to the heartwarming image of an infant swaddled and laid in a manger. Jesus offers life by sitting at the table with tax collectors and sinners, embracing children whom disciples would have shushed away, and seeking God's forgiveness for the very ones who crucify. Such is the life of Christ.

And therein resides the reason for choosing *zoe*, choosing life, as the word for the final letter. For where this book ends is where our discipleship begins—not just in Jesus' life but now in our living of the zoe Jesus promises. It is not enough to celebrate Christmas with carols and wreaths and stories that are then packed away for another year. The celebration of Christmas engages us in the life Jesus brings. As Jesus' life promised the peaceable kingdom, so our lives are to seek such peaceable ways in our times. As Jesus' life embraced and forgave and reconciled, so our lives are to embody such gracious ways. Jesus did not come simply that we might *have* life. Jesus came that we might *live* life.

Z is for *zoe*, for life. So live as God intended it. Live as Jesus embodied it. With grace. With love. With justice. With faithfulness. A blessed Christmas—and a blessed life—to you!

ENGAGING Zoe

For Families With Children

Pull out a dictionary and see how many words begin with the letters "zoo-." Notice how many of these words pertain to animals or life. Explain that the word *zoo* comes from the Greek word *zoe*, which means "life." Recall that at Christmas, we celebrate the new life or zoe that God promises to bring through Jesus.

Provide art materials and invite the children to create a mural that shows living things they see every day. Add photos or drawings of each child and talk about how wonderful it is to be alive and to be surrounded by so many living things.

For Couples or Friendship Groups

Create list of reasons to be grateful for life. Read John 10:10.

• What affirmation of life do you see in this verse?
• What images come to mind when you hear the phrase "life in its fullest"?
• How did Jesus embody life in its fullest?
• How might we follow his example and live out the zoe Jesus promised?

Watch the YouTube video "2010 West Volusia Young Life Cardboard Testimony" (http://youtu.be/U2q5TSKQ0uM).* Identify some of the ways the young people have experienced God's zoe.

• What would your cardboard testimony say?

Journal Exercise

What do you see God calling you to do in your life: today, this week, in the year to come? How will you draw upon God's grace and the support of others to translate those hopes into action? Write or draw your responses on page 127 of the journal section.

---

* All websites were accurate and functional at the time of publication. YouTube addresses are case sensitive

Outreach Project

Read Isaiah 58:6-7. How might these actions bring God's zoe to others? Decide on some actions you could take to bring life, justice, and hope to others in the coming year.

Devotional Activities

Read Revelation 22:1-2.

For Children: Invite the children to imagine that they are standing on the bank of the river that comes from God's throne. What can they see, hear, feel? Invite the children to help you prepare and taste a selection of fruit. (Be aware of allergies.) What do you think the fruit from the healing trees taste like? Play some lively music and ask the children to imagine that they are part of the river. Move through the whole house, bringing God's life, healing, and blessing into every corner.

For Adults: Where do you see God working to bring new life and healing? How might we be a part of that process? Where do you long to see God bring new life and healing? Provide paper leaf shapes large enough to act as bookmarks. Invite the participants to write their longings on one side and actions they might take to bring about that dream on the other. Have them place the leaves in their Bibles to use as bookmarks for the coming year.

Daily Prayer

Offer thanks for the life that God brought through Jesus. Ask the Spirit to help you live life to the fullest, as Jesus did.

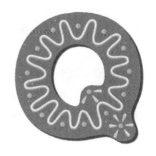

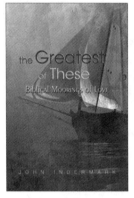

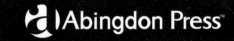